The Spirit of the Earth

The Spirit of the Earth

JOHN HART

paulist press new york/ramsey

Library of Congress
Catalog Card Number: 83-62015

ISBN: 0-8091-2581-1

Published by Paulist Press
545 Island Road, Ramsey, N.J. 07446

Printed and bound in the
United States of America

Contents

Introduction   1

chapter one
A Vanishing Land   7

chapter two
Mother Earth and God's Earth   41

chapter three
Pilgrims and Stewards   65

chapter four
An American Heritage   83

chapter five
The Church and the Land   105

chapter six
Land Reform   133

chapter seven
The Spirit of the Earth   149

Acknowledgements

A work such as this is impossible to create without the encouragement and assistance of a community of friends and associates. I would like to thank the Catholic bishops of heartland America for their confidence in me and encouragement of my work while I directed the Heartland Project. I thank also the Project Board and the people of the heartland for sharing their perceptions and visions. I am grateful to Jim Burns for suggesting this work and encouraging me during its development, to Phil Scharper for his support, and to Fr. Kevin Lynch and Doug Fisher, editors of Paulist Press, for facilitating its publication. Marty Strange of the Center for Rural Affairs in Walthill, Nebraska was kind enough to review and offer helpful comments on an earlier draft of Chapter One. Bonnie King and Eva Schenck typed most of the manuscript, at times tediously deciphering the words that emerged from my flying pen. And I thank Janie, my wife, and Shanti and Daniel, my children, for their loving patience and encouragement while I worked evenings and weekends at home.

for
Maurice Dingman:
friend,
Bishop
and
extraordinary
Christian

Introduction

*   *   *

Even the most casual observer driving through rural America could not fail to notice signs of its decline. Deserted and dilapidated farm buildings turn gray in rural fields. Empty and boarded stores line the streets of rural communities. The silence within homes, businesses, schools, and churches loudly proclaims that farmers and farmworkers alike have left rural areas to line up for welfare checks and food stamps in urban centers. Their money is gone, their hopes are shattered, their dreams have become nightmares.

Scenes of decay and despair such as these are common on highways and side roads across the country. From the corn-fields of the heartland to the cotton fields of the deep south, from the grape orchards of California to the apple orchards of New York, rural life and lives are dramatically and rapidly changing. The land is changing hands and its use is being altered in ways that at times do violence to it and to the people upon it.

As these changes occur, two basic questions are being asked by rural people: "Who should own the land?" and "How should the land be used?"

In an earlier day, such questions might have been answered simply: Those with political power or economic power or a pioneering spirit or a love of work—or any combination of these—should own the land. And their ownership should give them the right to do with their property whatever they wish.

But times have changed. We are more conscious today of the limited nature of our land base and of the fragile character

1

of the water and air that complement it. We know that the world's population is increasing at a rapid pace compared to previous eras. We see some segments of that population, particularly in the United States and western Europe, caught up in what seems to be at times a frenzy of consumerism, a frantic drive to deplete natural and human resources. We smell odors in the air we breathe and taste chemicals in the water we drink. We debate whether a given tract of land should remain a wheat field or become a suburban housing development or a new shopping mall. We demand cheap and plentiful food in a variety that defies local agricultural production and necessitates extensive and costly intranational and international shipping. And we see the family farm and the "mom and pop" grocery store disappear.

With this awareness, we see the questions of land ownership and use in a different light. We watch the evening news on television and notice that reports on the starving children in Cambodia and Brazil are interrupted by advertisements for pre-packaged foods; or we see news stories about gas lines in Washington and senior citizens freezing to death in Chicago, on a broadcast paid for in its entirety by one of the "seven sisters," the major oil companies that have come to dominate our economy and our lives. Then we wonder about this earth: "To whom do its resources belong?" and "How should they be used?"

If we have a biblical understanding of ourselves and of our relationship to God and to each other, we find the bases for our answers to our questions about land ownership and use in several biblical passages. In Leviticus we hear God tell the Israelites: "The land belongs to me, and to me you are strangers and guests" (25:23). In the Book of Psalms we are taught: "The Lord's are the earth and its fullness; the world and those who dwell in it" (24:1). We hear Jesus admonish us: "I was hungry and you did not feed me, thirsty and you gave me nothing to drink, naked and you clothed me not" (cf. Matthew 25). James questions us: "If a brother or sister has nothing to wear and no food for the day, and you say to them, 'God-bye and good luck! Keep warm and well fed,' but do not meet their bodily needs, what good is that?" (2:15–16); and Luke describes for us in Acts the lifestyle of the early Christian community: "Those who believed shared all things in common; they would sell their property and goods, dividing everything on the basis of each one's need" (2:44–45).

The contrast between ideal and reality can be brought home to us very dramatically, if only we have "eyes to see," if we have not become indifferent to the tragedy and suffering that confront us in the news media or in our own experiences.

Some years ago, while I was studying in Mexico, I was walking through the city of Querétaro, noted for its aqueduct and its colonial era churches. As I entered the courtyard of one of the latter, I saw at a distance a peasant woman kneeling on the rough stones, accompanied by her children. In the glare of the midday sun, I could not see what she was doing. I assumed that she was a pilgrim engaged in a practice common among pious poor people: traveling all or part of the distance from home to church on her knees as an act of penance. When I was close enough to see what she and her children were about, I was shocked and moved. Grain by grain they were gathering into burlap sacks the rice that earlier had been thrown at newlyweds. They were literally scraping up their evening meal from the fertility symbol commonly used at weddings. They would transform what was used as a symbol of life into a real life-giving substance. I asked myself then, and I have asked myself often since: Why should people be forced to meet their most basic needs in such desperation?

But hunger is a problem not only abroad, across an ocean or an artificial boundary line separating people from each other and into nations. Hunger is here, at home. I have seen Chicano children in south Texas crippled and retarded because of malnutrition and chemical sprays. I have seen black families in Washington thrown out of their homes because the apartments in which they lived for twenty years were to be converted into more profitable condominiums. I have heard Indian people in South Dakota, Montana, and Minnesota angrily protest being deprived of their land base, food sources, and culture. I have seen poor white people in Appalachia with faces drawn thin and tight by hunger. I have seen family farmers throughout the midwest worried about how they might provide for their family's needs with crop prices low and interest rates high.

My education and experiences have caused me to become a lifelong *activist,* committed to bringing about a more just social order. I see the activist role to be a combination of theory and practice, the utilization of the thinking function of the *academic* (who might live theory without action) and the activity function of the *agitator* (who might act without thinking). Theory and practice in unending tension are necessary components of an activist life. Without their interaction the world cannot be transformed. The academician's unactivated theory must be tested by the agitator's unreflective practice and vice versa.

In the face of the present reality of land relations, the biblical advocacy of caring for God's land and sharing of the land's goods might seem for some to be out of place, either an unrealizable ideal or merely the romantic dream of seers of a different age.

On the contrary. The biblical teachings present for us goals toward which we should strive and a lifestyle which we must live. The biblical affirmation that God suffers with and is one with the oppressed (see Mt 25:31–46) gives the poor hope—and gives middle class America food for thought in an intellectually and ethically starved culture.

The signs of hope are about us. We need only look more closely at the sharing and joyful celebrations of the poor, and at the occasional advocacy of their rights that comes from enlightened members of the church community, to see emerging a new understanding of God's mandate to the human family. This new understanding is that we who are "strangers and guests" upon the land, we who are sojourners on this earth, are called by God to be its stewards. We are to care for it and conserve it so that it might be "Mother Earth" (in the imagery of American Indians) and provide not only for our needs but also for the needs of our children.

The land is a sacred trust, given by God to our care. If we

are to be faithful to that trust, we must understand this earth and God's commands concerning it. We must try so to live in harmony with it and with all peoples that future generations might say of us that we walked gently on the earth and shared its bounty with each other.

If we examine our dual past as believers and as Americans we find some direction as to the theoretical and practical paths we must follow in order to care for this trust of land, this earth that, paradoxically in a nuclear age, both nourishes us and depends on us for its own life. In our past as believers we know through our Christian faith of the spirit of the earth, the God who brought it and ourselves into being. In our past as Americans we are linked to those who have lived here for centuries as the Americas' first human inhabitants, the American Indians, and so can come to learn from them of the spirit of the earth, the spirit of harmony that was celebrated also in the life of St. Francis of Assisi centuries ago.

What I hope to do in the pages that follow is to convey the urgency of the problems of land ownership and use, discuss the biblical perspective of stewardship and the American Indian understanding of our relationship with the earth, and set forth some proposals as to how we might work together to solve these problems, fulfill our stewardship responsibilities and live in harmony with the earth. Permeating these ideas is what is for me a sense and experience of the spirit of the earth and the Spirit of the earth.

In this book my primary focus for agricultural and American Indian issues is on heartland America, for that was my focus at the time of my writing. I describe the problems and reactions to them of heartland family farmers and plains Indians. I hope that from these particulars, though, a more universal understanding of and response to injustices on the land might be drawn. Family farmers across the nation are experiencing similar problems; American Indians throughout the country suffer similar injustices and hold similar perspectives; most of us, rural and urban people alike, share an attitude of respect for the Bible and its teachings; and all of us depend on the land for our very lives.

In this time of political turmoil, reflections on land issues of ownership and use are especially appropriate. Previous Democratic administrations did err, it is true, in social welfare allocations—but they erred on the side of the needy. Under Reaganomics, the administration is grossly erring—on the side of the greedy. In stark contrast to the Reagan "trickle down" policy that contradicts the religious and humanist American tradition and promotes family farm bankruptcies and hunger at home and starvation and social oppression and unrest abroad, we might consider the policy of King Agud of Persia in 996 A.D., a policy directly relevant (though perhaps not in its severity) to current questions of land ownership and use. The king decreed during a time of famine that for every poor person who died of starvation, a rich person would be executed. Thereafter, no one starved. We, too, must analyze our current situation of land ownership and use in the light of our traditions and the suffering of people in the United States and throughout the world, and respond accordingly.

I cannot develop at depth a theology of land and land ethics in the few pages of this book. I do hope to set forth some ideas with the hope that people who are unaware of problems of land ownership and use might become educated about them and inspired to work in their own contexts to resolve them, and that people who are aware of them might find here at least part of the theoretical base necessary for their ongoing labors to promote an equitable distribution of and care for the land and its resources.

In this spirit, let us begin our reflection on our trust of land. Let us explore our relationship to the Spirit of the earth.

chapter one

A Vanishing Land

*   *   *

A television commercial we frequently see, especially during the warm summer months, reminds us that orange juice "isn't just for breakfast anymore." This particular advertising is paid for by Florida citrus growers. When we go shopping in the grocery store located at the mall on the edge of town, we might smile in amusement if we recall that commercial when we take a can of orange juice from the frozen food section. What we do not realize is that the television commercial and our shopping trip are linked in more ways than just our purchase and consumption of orange juice.

Ironically, the place where we shop for the juice is representative of a nationwide trend toward dramatic changes in agricultural land use: prime agricultural land, the world's best land for food and fiber production, is being absorbed by urban and suburban development for such uses as shopping malls and the highways, streets, and parking lots necessary for using them. The end result is that in some states, according to projections by the United States Department of Agriculture (USDA), agricultural land will disappear entirely. Florida is among those states. The USDA projects that *all* of Florida's agricultural lands will disappear by the turn of the century if present trends continue. That means that in our lifetime or our children's lifetime, Florida orange juice will no longer be available. Today, the Florida citrus growers would have us consume their juice *more* than just at breakfast. Tomorrow, the Florida citrus growers will not even have lands on which to produce juice *just* for breakfast.

The case of Florida's citrus groves is but one example of vanishing land in the United States today. Across the nation land is disappearing physically, economically, and varietally.

Agricultural land is *physically* vanishing; it is being converted to non-agricultural use, it is being eroded by wind and water, and it is being devastated by acid rain and chemical dumping. Agricultural land is *economically* vanishing. Its ownership is becoming concentrated in fewer and fewer hands, while experienced farmers are forced off the land and aspiring farmers are denied access to the land. Finally, agricultural land is *varietally* vanishing. Its availability for farm diversity, genetic diversity, and basic food production is becoming more and more limited.

CONVERTED LAND

In areas surrounding the cities of rural America, a notice in the local newspaper that a new shopping center is opening usually makes most people only look eagerly to see what bargains will be offered for the week or so of the "grand opening." They note with approval that the new mall has "ample parking." They discover that it is "conveniently located": it is reached easily by a new cloverleaf interchange off the interstate highway. They do not realize that they are witnessing and unconsciously approving in miniature a problem that has reached the crisis stage during the past decade, the continuing and alarming loss to non-agricultural uses of some of the world's best agricultural land.

In 1981, the Census Bureau published new figures showing that between 1969 and 1978, U.S. agricultural lands decreased by eighty-eight million acres. This sharp decline in productive land took place in an era of rising food prices in the United States and rampant starvation and malnutrition around the world. The loss of agricultural land continues. Present conservative estimates are that at least *three million* acres are lost annually. Of that, about one million acres are prime agricultural land.

We who live in America have become accustomed to the word "million." The imagery used by the National Agricultural Lands Study makes us more aware of what a million acres might be. "A million acres equals a half-mile strip of land from New York to California—or the loss of four square miles of our best agricultural land every day" (from "Where Have the Farmlands Gone?").

Many of us might not be aware of just what is *prime* agricultural land. Prime farm land is the best land a farmer could have. It has excellent soil quality, is flat or slightly rolling, and is located in an area and climate that assure a long growing season with usually abundant moisture. Because of its quality characteristics, prime land assures high productivity and low energy use. About twenty-five percent of the world's prime agricultural land is located in the United States.

Prime farm land is not only the farmer's dream, it is the investor's dream as well, but for different reasons. The farmer looks on such land as a place to raise abundant crops and a family, a place where, compared to medium quality and marginal land, farming costs—equipment size, energy, fertilizer, conservation—will be relatively low and annual returns relatively high. The investor looks on such land as a place for potential urban or suburban development where, compared to hilly, rocky or wooded terrain, construction costs—clearing and leveling the land and installing necessary services—will be relatively low and the profit margin relatively high. In the ongoing battle for prime farmland, the farmer is increasingly the loser and the investor increasingly the winner.

Across the United States, then, bulldozers demolish barns and concrete displaces crops. A highway interchange might require one hundred and sixty acres of land. Rural highways in the U.S. cover about twenty-two million acres of land, consumed at the rate of about one hundred thousand acres yearly. A new subdivision might take "only" twenty to forty acres—

but, multiplied across the nation, the land absorbed yearly by new housing runs into the hundreds of thousands of acres. In the meantime, rural water supplies, vital for irrigation and food production in many areas, are being used up by industrial parks, residential swimming pools, nuclear reactor cooling systems, agribusiness centers, pivot irrigation systems, and coal slurry pipelines.

While the land is being paved over and the water supply runs dry, urban centers decay. Downtown shopping centers, with limited parking space taxed by parking meters, lose business to suburban malls and close down. Vacant buildings and vacant lots littered with broken glass and fallen bricks shelter shattered people with shattered dreams. Fire and health hazards abound. Economic victims become crime victims.

Agricultural land is being lost to the residential, commercial, and industrial wants of the cities not only by being paved over for malls, parking lots, homes, highways, airports, industrial parks and toxic chemical waste dump sites; energy demands absorb it as well. In some areas it is the search for and removal of fuel (oil, gas, coal, and uranium) that takes up the land; in other areas, coal-fired or nuclear power plants; in others, refineries for conversion of the raw material into fuel and by-products; in others, the network of power lines, often of a high voltage whose health impact on crops, livestock, and people is being questioned; in others, the disposal of toxic mine and plant wastes; and in yet others, a devastating combination of fuel availability, power production, power grids, and waste disposal. The land cries out for relief; people demand more energy. There is little evaluation of true energy *needs;* energy *wants* and the power companies' *greed* determine what additions to the energy production system are needed—even when an objective assessment indicates otherwise. In some areas, for example, energy needs were projected on an annual increase at a rate prevalent some years ago. That rate has dropped because of consumer conservation practices. Yet, the area power company pushes for eminent domain to purchase and develop land for power plants and lines. The company "logic" in some cases is that since a project has been started, it would be a waste of previously expended funds *not* to continue, instead of a waste of money to continue throwing good money after bad; in other cases this "logic" states that power is going to be cheaper in the area—despite the fact that construction costs will be passed on to the consumer. In yet other cases, "logic" seems to dictate that money resulting from higher than expected profits must be used for new construction rather than be rebated to the consumer or returned to the consumer by lower service rates. In all of this, rarely do the power companies and the government, through funding of research projects and pilot programs and technology, explore alternative, cleaner, less expensive energy sources: solar heating and cooling and electrical production and storage; wind-generated, geothermal (steam pressure from deep within the earth) and hydroelectric production of power; recycling of heat within a building; development of industrial filters and a recycling process for emission that would prevent pollution and waste from coal-fired plants; and a true evaluation of the *total* cost of a given energy form in order to educate the public about and produce the most cost- and energy-efficient systems. (Nuclear power, for example, is the most expensive and least efficient power source, besides having the greatest adverse effect on the environment. Yet industry and government work hand-in-hand to develop it, promote it, and impose it on the public.)

One of the worst devastaters of agricultural land and rural communities is the strip mine. In Appalachia, not only have the coal companies operating such mines destroyed farm land and areas of great natural beauty, but they have also, on occasion, uprooted the population of an entire town and bulldozed away homes, schools, churches, parks, and businesses in order to stripmine coal. In heartland America, the worst effects of coal stripmining might be seen on the prairies of Wyoming and in the meadows of Illinois. Ranchers with their cattle or sheep operations, and grassland flora and fauna, lose out in the first area mentioned; family grain and dairy farmers, and field and lake flora and fauna lose out in the second. In its well-researched study, "Who's Mining the Farm," the Illinois South Project describes land ownership and use problems in Illinois:

> The State of Illinois is one of the nation's leading agricultural states. It leads the nation in the production of corn and soybeans, and is also the top-ranking exporter of agricultural goods. Over 81% of the total land base is in farms. . . .
>
> The state has coal resources totaling 161 billion tons. This coal is spread throughout 86 of the state's 102 counties, and underlies 65% of the total land surface. The State currently ranks fourth among the nation's coal-producing states. . . .
>
> *Our land ownership research documented almost 380,000 acres of Illinois land in the hands of coal companies in 1977–1978* (emphasis in original).

The study indicates further that much of the wealth from coal mining goes to a minority of companies, most of which are subsidiaries of oil companies and other transnational (operating in many countries) corporations. The eleven largest companies (of a total of twenty-eight) accounted in 1977 for ninety-seven and a half percent of the total coal production in the state. Despite all their wealth and laws requiring land restoration, the coal companies often have to be pressured by local public interest groups before they try to relieve some of the devastation of the land.

In Illinois, then, the "food versus fuel" issue is dramatically evident. We shall see later other ways in which this controversy pits rural farmers against urban consumers—often unnecessarily.

The loss of prime farm land means more than suburban development and urban decay, more than energy development and agricultural destruction. It also means that farmers must turn to less suitable land to produce their crops. Poorer soil requires heavier fertilizer inputs, which means pollution of the land and water and health hazards for farm families, their neighbors, and urban consumers. Poorer soil is more susceptible to wind erosion which helps destroy the land base. Poorer land requires heavier machinery which needs more fuel and helps deplete energy resources and drive up fuel prices. Poorer land must be irrigated more, and so uses up more of the water base. Poorer land, then, requires greater outlays and inputs than prime land for the same production. And it cannot as easily be divided among farm children to serve as their initial base of entry into farming, because its low overall quality and consequent lower productivity mean that it cannot support newly expanded families as easily as prime lands; it cannot support as many individuals or families, when divided by inheritance into smaller subsections, as can an equal amount of prime agricultural land.

Conversion of the land, then, forces farmers from their homes and work, contributes to urban decay, accelerates land erosion, depletes water reserves, promotes pollution of air, land, and water and calls into question the ability of the United States to feed its people (while the U.S. is losing twelve square miles of land daily, its projected need is a sixty to eighty-five percent increase in demand for the land's products. Besides Florida, New Hampshire and Rhode Island are also expected to lose one hundred percent of their agricultural land by the year 2000).

ERODED LAND

Most of us have seen, either first-hand or through the media, farmlands devastated by drought and erosion in the 1930's during the Great Depression. For some of us, it is painful to recall the Dust Bowl conditions of the past. We remember our suffering, the sense of hopelessness we shared with our parents, the pain of hunger, the sting of blowing sand on our faces. For others of us, the memory of the photographs that we have seen might trigger a vague curiosity about just what happened and why. In either case, we are aware of the tragedy of that era, and grateful that we do not suffer its pain today.

We do not realize that, in some agricultural areas, dust bowl conditions are developing. We do not realize that, even where a dust bowl will not occur, land is being drastically eroded.

In most cases, soil erosion is caused by poor farming practices that heighten the effects of water and wind on the land. In the first installment of his Pulitzer prize-winning series, "Environmental Crisis Down On The Farm," James Risser of the *Des Moines Register* wrote that above the entrance to Union Station in Washington, D.C., amid statements about American industry, there is the inscription:

> The Farm—best home of the family, main source of national wealth, foundation of civilized society, the natural providence.

Risser then observes that a cynic might add:

> The Farm—destroyer of the soil, fouler of the nation's waters, threat to the public health, the great polluter." ("Pollution, Soil Losses Cause Alarm," *Des Moines Register,* September 10, 1978.)

After studying for six months the impact of agriculture on the environment, Risser concluded that the U.S. high agricultural production came "at a high cost to the country's natural environment," and that "an ecological crisis may be brewing." He soberly noted:

> Not only is agriculture one of the leading causes of water pollution in the U.S., but it is destroying much of the precious soil its continued success depends on.

Risser's assessment complements that of the Soil Conservation Society of America (SCSA), a non-profit scientific and educational association concerned about conserving land and water resources. In the Foreword to SCSA's book *Soil Conser-*

vation Policies: An Assessment, Lyle Bauer, president of the National Association of Conservation Districts wrote:

> This could well mark a historic turning point in our nation's use and treatment of natural resources. We appear to be entering an entirely new era, one in which the scarcity of land and water may, for the first time, be an important factor in our national economy and, consequently, in our national policy.

In a similar vein, William C. Moldenhauer, SCSA's president, stated in the book's Preface:

> Soil is worth saving. We must keep making this point again and again. Making the point becomes more and more difficult as society becomes more urban oriented and many people think of milk as coming from the supermarket instead of the cow.

The reason that knowledgeable people are concerned about the physical loss of our rural land base through erosion is that the loss is occurring at a rate that many experts view as alarming. They realize, as most Americans and even most farmers do not realize, that today *agricultural land loses more topsoil each year than it lost in the worst years of the Dust Bowl era.* Thus, words that Franklin D. Roosevelt uttered in 1937 should be a warning to us today more than when he said them: "The nation that destroys its soil destroys itself."

The soil is being destroyed from two directions: prime agricultural land is being converted to non-agricultural uses; fair and marginal agricultural lands are being eroded by wind and water because of poor conservation practices. The heart of the matter is that some farmers or potential farmers are being forced from prime land to marginal land by urban developers and then, caught in a cost-price squeeze (high prices paid out for seed, fertilizer and other chemicals, land and equipment, and high interest rates when borrowing money; low prices coming in for farm products) try to work the poorer soil to produce at a level comparable to better soil. Thus, they use more chemicals and heavier equipment and set aside such conservation practices as contour plowing, terraces, shelterbelts (wind breaks of trees) and grass waterways.

The end result is accelerated erosion. U.S. farms lose an average of nine tons of soil per acre annually—and new topsoil is created at the rate of only four tons per acre annually. And the soil that is washed off the farm and into rivers and streams is not only a loss to agriculture, it becomes a health hazard as well, for it contains chemical residues from herbicides, pesticides, and fertilizers. People and animals that drink the water, and fish that swim in it, are the unwitting health casualties of agricultural decline. So, too, are bodies of water that become biologically dead. High crop yields are purchased at the price of water quality.

Soil erosion is a serious problem in an age of population increases and food scarcity. In Iowa, a state which produces ten percent of the U.S. food supply and twenty percent of its food exports, agronomists note that for every bushel of corn produced two bushels of soil are lost. Iowa is in danger of losing more than *half* of its cropland from water erosion alone. The implications for consumers (higher prices) and the world's hungry (food scarcity) are enormous. Thus, soil erosion is a problem that affects both urban and rural people, even though the former have little or no contact with the land. What they "don't know" *can* hurt them down the road.

CORRODED LAND

In mid-November 1980, rural residents throughout the U.S. were awakened at night by the sound of heavy trucks roaring through the countryside. During the same period, owners of urban warehouses, railroad tank cars, and truck tank trailers discovered that individuals or companies that had rented their property had disappeared without a trace. The rural citizenry and urban businesspeople soon discovered the reason for these mysterious goings on: toxic chemical wastes were being dumped on highways, in streams, and on fields, or left in rented storage, to beat the November 19 deadline for the imposition of new federal regulations governing toxic waste disposal.

Industrial waste disposal is one factor in corrosion of the land. Urban wastes also corrode the land. So, too, does the acid rain that falls on the crops and cities of the midwest and Canada, and the radioactivity from nuclear wastes stored around the U.S.

In an article appearing in the *Kansas City Times* series "The Land: Will It Last?" and entitled "Hazardous Waste Is Fine—In Someone Else's Back Yard," Robert Engelman observes that toxic waste

> poses some of the most difficult land abuse questions to face an industrialized society: Can any means to store highly toxic substances really protect the land for hundreds or thousands of years?

Advocates of regulated sites claim that they can, and point to sites having no leaks. Opponents, especially people living near actual or proposed dump sites, question whether or not that is so, and point to Love Canal as a prime example of what happens to people and the land, or discuss former forest areas denuded by chemical wastes, agricultural lands that have become sludge ponds, and the odor and taste of their drinking water.

The threat of acid rain to fields, forests, and bodies of water is relatively new. Acid rain is rain falling from clouds contaminated by smoke from fossil fuels burned by homes, factories, and power plants. The combination of pollutants and water causes a chemical reaction whose product is a strong acid. (In Minnesota, for example, the acidity of acid rain is ten times higher than that of natural precipitation.) This acid falls on fields and decimates crops, on forests and depletes timber reserves, and on lakes and kills fish. (In Canada, half of whose acid rain comes from the United States, the fish population of one hundred and forty lakes has been wiped out. That of an additional forty-eight thousand lakes could suffer the same fate in two decades.) In cities, too, people feel the sting of acid rain on their skin and see its corrosive effect on auto and home paint.

The land is being corroded by our chemicals and our acid rain. This corrosion is another factor contributing to the loss of our land base.

CONSOLIDATED LAND

In an ironic reversal of a bygone era, barns are being torn down across rural America. Sometimes, if they are not very old and their wood is still good, they might be taken apart piece by piece by a carpenter seeking to salvage material for another project, who realizes that the quality of the wood (in both tree type and curing process) is far superior to that commercially available today. At other times, if they are the appropriate shade of gray that results from the farmer's poverty and the weather's severity, their siding is bought for resale by an interior designer or other urban (or suburban) resident interested in paneling a wall in a living room or a den. In the worst of times, the barn is simply demolished by a bulldozer or crane and its remnants hauled away to the local dump site. The ironic reversal is that people once gathered together at the farm either of a new neighbor or of the son or daughter of an old neighbor, to build as a community a barn that represented, for a beginning farmer, a commitment to the land in the present and hope for ongoing stability, security, and stewardship in the future.

Tragically for rural America, barn-raising has been replaced by barn demolition. That physical change highlights other physical changes and an attitudinal change. Farms are growing larger and farther apart, and their separation in space represents and contributes to their separation in spirit. Neighbors are no longer neighbors; the spirit of community of lives and of purpose is disappearing. Individual wants blind people from seeing and serving community needs.

Farm size is increasing and farm families are decreasing.

According to studies by the United States Department of Agriculture, the average size of a farm in the United States more than doubled in less than thirty years, from 213 acres in 1950 to 435 acres in 1978. The result has been that a smaller and smaller percentage of farms have a larger and larger percentage of acres owned and income received. The largest farms—those with a thousand acres or more—although only constituting 6.6 percent of the total number of farms, contain 54.1 percent of the total land of all farms. Or, looked at another way, farms having more than $100,000 in gross sales comprise only seven percent of all farms but receive thirty-six percent of the net farm income. The figures for *all* land owned are even more lopsided: one percent of the owners of all the private land in the United States own almost fifty percent of that land. (In farmland, one percent of all owners own 30.3 percent of all farmland.) On the other end of the scale, seventy-five percent of the owners of all private land in the United States own only three percent of the land. The trend, according to USDA, is toward "a gradual disenfranchisement, a separation, of the majority of the people from the land . . ." moving agriculture "from a nation of many small businesses to a nation of a few large firms and many wage-earners" (from *A Time to Choose: Summary Report on the Structure of Agriculture*).

In 1920 farm families comprised 30.1 percent of the total population. Thirty years later, in 1950, that number had dropped to 15.3 percent. Another thirty years brought the farm population down to 2.8 percent of the total population. The figures for numbers of farms during those years reveal the trend toward consolidation. In 1920 there were 6.5 million family farms; in 1949 there were 5.7 million, and in 1979 there were 2.3 million. The figures become startling when we consider that between 1920 and 1949, while the United States endured all the hardship of the Great Depression and World War II, 800,000 farms disappeared. But then, during the post-war period of prosperity for the rest of America, 3.4 million disappeared. And, for every six farms that disappeared during those years, one rural business followed. Meanwhile, rural schools and churches closed because of the declining population and the consequent loss of their economic support base, and urban areas were pressed to provide jobs or welfare payments for the displaced rural unemployed and education for their children.

The consolidation of farmland has been advocated by government and agribusiness alike, and fostered by such factors as inflation, cheap food, government tax policies, and a bias, on the part of most land grant colleges and county extension agents, toward large scale operators. But it has no firm theoretical or practical base in terms of benefits to the land, to agriculture in general, to rural communities, or to consumers. For example, decaying farmhouses, boarded storefronts, empty school playgrounds, and silent church steeples in rural areas, and higher unemployment, longer welfare lines, higher crime rates, and poorer quality food in urban areas all result from the decline in family farms. Two studies bear mentioning here: the Department of Agriculture's own, entitled "The One-Man Farm" (1973), and Walter Goldschmidt's classic analysis of California agriculture, originally prepared for (but suppressed by) the Bureau of Agricultural Economics of the USDA, later printed by the Senate Subcommittee on Small Business and recently published as the book, *As You Sow.*

"The One-Man Farm" study was developed to determine what technically optimum farms might be throughout the U.S. The size would vary, of course, depending on such factors as soil quality, climate, available water, and crop planted. The USDA determined that "the fully mechanized one-man farm, producing the maximum acreage of crops of which the man and his machines are capable, is generally a technically efficient farm." The "technically optimum one-man farm" proposed by the USDA "is larger, requires more capital, and demands a higher level of managerial talent than is found on most one-man farms today in the United States." Thus, the USDA is advocating larger farms overall. However, it is still advocating an operation under one person's management, a person who is the owner-operator of the farm and does most of the labor on it (together with family members). Therefore, while the general thrust of the USDA (except during the relatively brief term of Bob Bergland as Secretary during the Carter administration) was toward promoting "more efficient" agribusinesses and assisting the efforts of agribusiness corporations, the "one-man farm" study noted in contrast that "the chief incentive for farm enlargement beyond the optimum one-man size is not to reduce unit costs of production, but to achieve a larger business, more output, and more total income." The study points out:

> We are so conditioned to equate bigness with efficiency that nearly everyone assumes that large-scale undertakings are inherently more efficient than smaller ones. In fact, the claim of efficiency is commonly used to justify bigness. But when we examine the realities we find that most of the economies associated with size in farming are achieved by the one-man fully mechanized farm. Farms larger than "optimum" are essentially multiples of the optimum farm, and are technically no more efficient than the one-man farm.

In a small way, then, the USDA acknowledged that the extensive land holdings that have become characteristic of American agriculture are not the optimum efficient units (part of the Department's bias is still present, however, in the size it chooses for the "one-man farm," and its emphasis on mechanization).

In 1944, the USDA's Bureau of Agricultural Economics suppressed publication of a study it had commissioned on the contrasting impacts on rural communities of family farms and agribusiness ventures. The USDA apparently commissioned the study to have a theoretical justification for its advocacy of the benefits of large-scale agribusiness over small-scale agriculture. Dr. Walter Goldschmidt, who made the study, came to the opposite conclusion: he showed the greater benefits of family farm agriculture.

Goldschmidt compared two towns: Arvin, surrounded by corporate farms, and Dinuba, surrounded by family farms. Both were about the same size, in areas of comparable climate and topography, and influenced by equivalent economic factors, with the exception of farm sizes.

Thirty years after his study, in 1972, Professor Gold-schmidt (now at UCLA) summarized his findings in testimony before U.S. Senator Fred Harris' hearings on the monopoly of land in California:

> Though the total dollar volume of agricultural production was the same, the communities differed in the following important ways:
>
> - The small farm community (Dinuba) had more institutions for democratic decision-making and a much broader participation in such activities by its citizenry.
>
> - The small farms supported about twenty percent more people and at a measurably higher level of living.
>
> - The majority of the small farm community population were independent entrepreneurs, as against less than twenty percent in the large farm community, where nearly two-thirds were agricultural wage laborers.
>
> - The small farm community in all instances had better community facilities: more schools, more parks, more newspapers, more civic organizations, and more churches.
>
> - The small farm community (Dinuba) had twice as many business establishments as the large-farm town (Arvin) and did sixty-one percent more retail business, especially in household goods and building equipment.
>
> - Physical facilities for community living—paved streets, sidewalks, garbage disposal, sewage disposal, and other public services—were far greater in the small-farm community; indeed, in the industrial-farm community, some of these facilities were entirely wanting. . . .
>
> The thesis of the study is that industrialized farming creates an urban pattern of social organization. . . . In California, we had created a new kind of agriculture, based upon extensive holdings, heavy mechanization and capitalization, and above all on the existence of a large class of laborers. . . . Clearly the study revealed precisely those

differences that are expressed in the theory of urbanization: increased differentials in social status and class distinctions, impoverishment, the absence of social ties based upon sentiment and the substitution of wages instead, a general lack of participation in the social system by the majority of the people, and a sense of alienation among them.

Goldschmidt concluded that if present trends continue, "rural communities as we have known them will cease to exist." He added:

Instead, the landscape will be dotted by what can be called company towns, made up of workers and overseers, together with such service personnel as the company chooses not to provide itself.

The condition of California is becoming, unfortunately, the condition of heartland America as well. The prospect seems to be for a rather grim future, if things remain unchanged. Goldschmidt's findings might be summarized to read that the people of Arvin (and similar towns) suffer from lack of property, lack of self-esteem, lack of community, and lack of democracy. This, then, is where the consolidation of agricultural lands will take the rest of rural America. Its effect on urban America will be higher priced but nutritionally lower, chemically poisoned, and ever more tasteless food.

OVERWORKED LAND

Those of us who cross America by airplane sometimes can see uses and abuses of the land from a broader perspective than can people on the ground, especially those who work the land and are caught up in the struggle to satisfy their particular needs and wants. They might tend to have a more limited view of the overall picture: they might indeed believe in conservation, for example, but lack either the financial resources or the concern for the land necessary to implement conservation practices. In our flight we might see examples of several ways in which the land is overworked: bare patches in a corn field betray the intense cultivation that does not allow the soil to regenerate itself; hillsides replete with logs and lacking new tree plantings reveal shortsighted forestry practices; green circles of crops interspersed with brown and barren circles of land demonstrate poor planning in the installation of, and water depletion because of, center pivot irrigation systems; and cattle or sheep foraging restlessly on a field containing barely more than the stubble of vegetation indicates overgrazing of rangeland. All of these scenes reveal to us an increasing problem in rural America: the overworking of the land and of the water that complements it.

Since the days when corn was first introduced to European immigrants by indigenous peoples, its uses have been creatively expanded. From corn meal to corn on the cob, from corn for people to corn for livestock, from popcorn to corn oil, from margarine to alcohol for people to alcohol for automobiles, we have learned to make corn part of our lives in a variety of almost indispensable ways. Farmers work hard to satisfy our demand for corn, a demand which, in part, they helped create.

Our demand for corn has meant that some farmers or agribusiness corporations plant corn from fence row to fence row and for season after season. This is an unfortunate occurrence, because corn depletes the soil of nitrogen at a very high rate. In the past, when the depth of topsoil was greater and when farmers rotated their crops, left a field fallow for a season, or alternated corn with nitrogen-restoring alfalfa, the soil was able to regenerate itself. Today the quest for profit or survival does not allow such stewardship of the soil. The result is that the soil, depleted of its natural nutrients, must be saturated with chemicals. Eventually it becomes packed and dry, and not even nitrogen-based chemicals can coax a crop from it. Such chemicals, at any rate, have a side-effect of their own: they leach through the soil into aquifers (natural underground water reservoirs) or are carried into rivers and streams by wind and rain. In both cases cancer-causing nitrites find their way into urban and rural drinking water. Erosion, too, results from depletion of soil nutrients. Thus the bare patches in the cornfield do not ordinarily mean that the corn planter missed some spots. They mean that the earth is dying in those places and, potentially, in the rest of the field as well. While the soil is dying, people must be concerned about the cancer-causing chemicals used to continue its productivity. When the soil is dead, people will have to worry about satisfying their hunger. In either case, depletion of soil nutrients has to do with human survival.

Occasionally when an urban nursery has a sale on trees, it might have in its window or in its newspaper advertisement the suggestion to "plant a walnut tree for your grandchildren." The meaning of this message is that a walnut tree takes long years to grow, and that it will be fully mature only in our grandchildren's time. It is a valuable hardwood as well, and so our grandchildren will be able to reap financial advantage from it.

The advertising line might be food for thought in other ways. It suggests to us that a forest of trees also takes time to grow—and so, by extension of that perception, we are told that we must carefully cultivate and conserve our forests, which might take eighty or a hundred years to regenerate themselves. That message is being heard by some people in the lumber industry. However, not all corporations (despite heavily financed and beautiful commercials to the contrary) conserve the forests under their care. Extensive spraying of chemicals on forest areas reduces the variety of trees available (the quick-growing, quickly profitable pine, for example, is preferred over longer growing hardwoods, and so a broadleaf herbicide related to the infamous Agent Orange used in Vietnam is sprayed over forests to eliminate trees other than pines)—and poses health hazards to birds, fish, animals, and people. In forestry practices, then, the earth is being overworked. The results of intensive timbering are erosion, health problems, and varietal depletion.

The green circles that create a patchwork quilt on the Great Plains states are the result of a relatively new form of irrigation, the center pivot irrigation system. Invented by Frank Zybach in 1949, the center pivot system has enabled crops to be grown in part of an area once called the "Great American Desert." The center pivot system consists of horizontal sections of pipe, on wheels, hooked up to the pump on an irrigation well. A motor drives the apparatus forward, so that it gradually moves in a circle over a field dispensing water and, in some cases, herbicides, pesticides, and fertilizers. For a while now, it has seemed that the biblical prophecy that "the desert shall bloom" has become a reality. But a careful observation of the effects of center-pivot systems (some of which are a half-mile long) and an analysis of their impact on aquifers supplying essential water to farms and cities for residential, commercial, and industrial uses caution against such an optimistic appraisal.

In some areas, center-pivot systems have been installed with poor planning in the rush for a quick profit. Some land which was plowed and irrigated had no chance of sustaining agricultural operations. It now is eroded and barren. The plow broke the plains by removing natural prairie grasses that survived and prospered for millennia. With neither crops nor cover, the land was susceptible to wind and water erosion. In other areas, the proliferation of the systems is the problem. Water is being drawn from the aquifers at a rate ten times their ability to replenish themselves. Farms and cities are in danger of losing their water supplies. Farmers and ranchers who install them are facing difficulties as well. Those who purchased them decades ago assumed that a given depth for the well would be sufficient to meet their needs. However, the great number of systems has lowered the aquifer below that point, and so they must either expend money to deepen their system or go out of business. The problems of center-pivot systems are especially acute in Nebraska, which leads the nation in acreage (2.4 million acres) irrigated by them. The systems are drawing down water from the Ogallala aquifer that underlies parts of eight Great Plains states. The aquifer is unable to recharge itself to meet the demand. Therefore, some agronomists are predicting that within a decade parts of Nebraska (and of Kansas and Texas as well) will have Dust Bowl conditions equal to or surpassing those of the "Dirty Thirties."

The center-pivot systems are not the only form of irrigation depleting water supplies. More traditional types of systems are having a similar effect. Rivers are being diverted by increasing numbers of farmers or in increasing volumes by existing farmers. The result in some cases is that the remaining water has a higher salt concentration. This means that further down the river the supply and quality of drinking water and irrigation water are diminished. People might become accustomed to the salty taste of their water, but irrigated crops cannot make a similar adjustment and have lower yields.

For reasons such as these, the *Kansas City Times* entitled a series of articles about the water issue "The Next American Crisis" (May 11–16, 1981). In this series the *Times* noted that *the Ogallala Aquifer, which supplies water for twenty-five percent of the nation's irrigated farmland,* "is dying, slowly, surely, bleeding to death." When the center-pivots were introduced thirty years ago, only two thousand wells tapped the Ogallala. Today, some seventy thousand tap it, and there are virtually no limits on new entries. The result is going to be as follows:

> Within twenty years, irrigated acreage will decline by half in the High Plains. By century's end, Kansas alone faces the loss of two million irrigated acres. . . . And by 2020, virtually all irrigation water in Kansas will be gone. With such a significant portion of America's dinner table dependent on the Ogallala, eventually the depletion could spur higher food prices and the loss of thousands of jobs in irrigated agriculture.

The seemingly unlimited supply of water has benefited agriculture in the Plains states for some thirty years now. But the time has come for significant measures to be employed to prevent the "boom" from becoming a "bust." If the water balloon should burst, the dreams and schemes and lives and livelihoods of many Americans will be adversely affected.

In our flight across rural America we also noted the restless foraging of livestock indicative of overgrazed land. Today, some one hundred and fifty million acres of rangeland—most of it on federal property leased at low rates to ranchers—suffer from this problem. Here, as in other cases of overworking the land, the earth has no opportunity to regenerate itself. This means that the livestock feeding on the vegetation deplete it to such an extent that it becomes increasingly sparse, and ultimately disappears. Then, without its grass cover, the soil is washed or blown away, making regeneration even more difficult, if not impossible. Ranchers attracted by low fees on federal lands and lacking a sense of responsibility for those lands (even though they are public lands, meant for and paid by the taxes of all of the public, including ranchers) allow their livestock to damage the earth while they save the few dollars more that it would cost them for additional lands sufficient to meet the needs of their herds or flocks; then they move their livestock on to overgraze another area.

In a number of ways, then, the land is overworked. Its ability to help meet the basic food and fiber needs of the global human family is diminished. A similar problem arises because of the homogeneity of crops grown in some areas.

HOMOGENOUS LAND

In 1980, the Presidential Commission on World Hunger predicted a major world food crisis by the year 2000. Most Americans hardly took notice of the report issued by the Commission, which suggested that the U.S. government should strengthen nutritional programs for America's poor and "make the elimination of hunger the primary focus of its relationships with the developing countries." The report was pretty well ignored by the Carter administration; it has been effectively dismissed by the Reagan administration. Under both administrations, the U.S. government has subordinated concern for the hungry to corporate and military welfare programs. Big business and the Pentagon are the primary recipients of government handouts. It is a case of profits before people and guns before butter.

Government abdication of responsibility for the poor is a reflection of an overall societal view. Conservative propaganda has been effective in convincing Americans that most welfare people "cheat" and most unemployed people are "lazy."

In the area of agriculture, public policy and private practices also are geared away from food needs and family farm survival and toward profit margins and agribusiness corporations. That orientation is evident in the ways in which land is used across the nation. There is a growing homogenization of the land—a tendency away from agricultural diversification and toward monoculture, away from genetic diversification and toward a limited seed base, and away from provision diversification and toward pecuniary production.

In days past, most family farmers had diversified operations. Besides planting such crops as corn and beans, they raised chickens for eggs and meat, cows for milk, and hogs for meat. They also used horses for plowing, or, as time went on, a combination of horses and small tractors. They fed their animals with grain they grew themselves and used their animals' manure for fertilizer.

Gradually, however, this diversification has been giving way in many areas to monoculture, the production of a single crop (such as corn) or of a single type of agriculture (such as grains in general or crops in general). In a diversified operation, farmers did not have to rely on one product for their livelihood—if corn prices were down, dairy prices might be up, and vice versa. With monoculture however, farmers were dependent on the market for their survival—a drastic drop in prices could mean disaster. Homogeneity in this sense means, then, loss of agricultural diversification.

In a *Washington Post* editorial from 1979, another homogenous practice is highlighted: the gradual loss of genetic diversification in the crops that are planted. In the editorial, entitled "Seeds of Trouble," the *Post* noted:

> For some years now, geneticists and agricultural planners have worried about the worldwide loss of genetic diversity among plant crops. . . . It holds the potential for true biological disaster. . . .

The editorial goes on to describe how "fewer and fewer varieties of crops" are being planted. For example, only six varieties of corn account for seventy-one percent of corn acreages. The "biological disaster" that could take place is the complete destruction of *all* of the nation's corn (or wheat, or tomatoes) should a pest or disease or climatic change occur. What has happened is that most of the seed planted is hybrid: developed over a short period of time in laboratories and experimental fields. The plants have not stood the test of time in dealing with natural enemies. In the quest for larger and more fruitful plants, scientists may have bred out resistance characteristics. And today, most varieties of a given plant are closely related, often hybrids of the same hybrid, produced for high yields. Thus, a disease or pest attacking one could quickly spread; a dramatic change in climate could have a devastating effect on all the plants of a particular crop. The National Academy of Science has observed that "most crops are impressively uniform genetically and impressively vulnerable." Some scientists have traveled to Latin America in search of non-hybrid seeds to establish a "seed bank" but found that some U.S. multinational companies either have sold hybrid seed to farmers there, or have bought agricultural lands and planted hybrids on them.

The problems of genetic homogenization are heightened further by present and proposed "seed patent laws," which permit the owner of a patented hybrid to determine who shall be able to plant it and grow it. Moreover, such owners (or their customers) might be able to prevent (as is the case in England, one of the nations pioneering in seed patent laws) a non-patented variety from being planted in areas adjacent to those having patented seeds, so that the latter might not be subject to cross-pollination. Hence, patent owners can effectively control not only who will plant their seed—but also who will plant *any* seed. Those who own the patents, then, will be able to control national and global food supplies. Multinational corporations are well aware of the potential power involved in seed patent laws. Purex, ITT, Shell and Union Carbide, to cite just a few, have recently purchased such major seed companies as Burpee and Northrup-King, as well as lesser known companies. Corporate control of agriculture is thus extended a step further toward complete dominance.

Homogenization of agriculture is also evident in the trend from provision diversification to pecuniary production. In an earlier era farmers, who were usually owner-operators, looked upon the land as a resource to enable them to meet the food needs of their immediate family and of the broader human family; the farm was to provide life and livelihood. Today, however, the attitude engendered by agribusiness corporations is that the land is to serve the pecuniary interests of the landowner. Thus, the twofold understanding of providing for one's own and others' needs has been condensed into one object: providing for one's own needs and wants, with minimal concern about others' hunger. (For some farmers, the basic issue might be survival, escaping from the cost-price squeeze.)

We have seen already the abuse of the land caused by such selfishness. It is also present when crops are raised for profit and not to meet people's needs. People living on the east coast, for example, have discovered in recent years that large, round, soft, delicious and nutritious tomatoes are hard to find. Instead, small, square-sided, hard, bland, and nutritionally deficient tomatoes are offered in supermarket produce departments. These tomatoes, like hybrid seeds, are the invention of scientists doing research, usually in universities, for corporate agriculture. They were developed to meet two profit needs: displacement of workers by machinery and lowering of shipping costs. When mechanization of tomato harvesting began, owners soon realized that a metal machine could not pick tomatoes with the gentle touch of the human hand, nor could it discern degrees of ripeness. So, a hard tomato had to be developed that could endure the mechanical harvester's grasp, and green tomatoes had to be colored for sale. Hard tomatoes were developed, and then gassed with nitrous oxide to change their skin color. Then someone noticed that square objects pack more easily into square holes than round objects do. So, hybrid tomatoes were developed that had square sides to pack more easily into boxes. As these developments took place, tomatoes had bred out of them taste, texture, and nutritional value. (Similar types of genetic manipulation have been attempted in other areas of agricultural production as well. Some scientists, determining that more chicken lovers preferred white meat to dark meat, tried to develop a very large-breasted chicken. However, the unfortunate birds were too top heavy, nor could they mate properly. Then there were the scientists who tried to develop a featherless chicken in order to save plucking costs. But poultry farmers had to turn up the heat to keep them warm, thus having higher energy costs, while the birds were excitable and prone to ulcers.)

Finally, pecuniary production's dominance over food needs is seen in extensive tobacco acreages. Land which might better be used for basic food is utilized for a superfluous luxury, one whose adverse health effects require a warning label on cigarette packs. The food that gives life is displaced by the tobacco that takes life. In the meantime, government and private research groups seek a cure for lung cancer instead of the obvious preventive for most of it, elimination of tobacco, its primary cause. Despite the social costs of people's hunger and people's health, tobacco field owners not only retain that use of their lands, they also get a break in the nation's agriculture programs. In the 1981 Farm Bill, for example, while price supports for other agricultural products such as milk, corn, and wheat were raised minimally to offset inflation, tobacco received generous support. Thus, while one government agency spends millions in advertising to curtail smoking because of its cancer potential, and government-supported research seeks a cure for cancer, Congress appropriates money to promote the cause of cancer.

CONTAMINATED LAND

On March 28, 1979 residents of the city of Harrisburg, Pennsylvania and its surrounding rural areas awoke to some startling news: the Three Mile Island nuclear power plant had suffered a partial meltdown, and a state of emergency had been declared at the plant. Although state and federal officials said initially that there was no cause for alarm, within the next twenty-four hours people would learn that radioactive gases had leaked into the air, and Pennsylvania's Governor Richard Thornburgh declared:

> I am advising those who may be particularly susceptible to the effects of radiation, that is, pregnant women and school-age children, to leave the area within a five-mile radius of the Three Mile Island facility until further notice.

That evening and over the next several days displaced families huddled in sports arenas and school gymnasiums, wondering not only if they could ever return to their homes and jobs but also if they had already received harmful doses of radiation. Their concern was expressed graphically in T-shirts some would soon be wearing which said: "I survived Three Mile Island—I think."

The people of rural York and Lancaster counties, like most people in Pennsylvania and the United States, had accepted the advent of nuclear power with enthusiasm. After all, it was supposed to be safe and a source of cheap energy in a nation that was dependent on foreign oil to meet its high energy consumption. Besides, it provided numerous local jobs during plant construction and a lesser number during operation. For such people, the smoking cones of Three Mile Island were evidence of a much harsher reality. For the first time, too, newspapers, television networks and individual citizens began to take a much closer look not only at nuclear power plants but also at the whole nuclear fuel cycle, from mining through power production and into waste disposal. Many came to realize to their shocked surprise that throughout that nuclear cycle the land was being contaminated and the health of its inhabitants was being threatened.

Harmful radiation effects begin right with uranium mining. The primary adverse mining effects are lung cancer, caused by escaping radon gas, and pulmonary fibrosis, caused by the implantation of particles of silica dust in the lungs. As a group, the people suffering most at this stage of the nuclear process are the Navajo Indians who do much of the mining: the world's largest uranium production comes from northwestern New Mexico, and nearly forty-seven percent of the uranium comes from land on Indian reservations.

After mining, the uranium ore is milled and refined. Its residue, called tailings, is often piled in huge artificial hills on open ground. The radioactive particles are blown by the wind across fields and so into homes and businesses and people's food and lungs, and washed by rain into water systems used by people, wildlife and farm animals. Also, radon gas is emitted from the tailings for generations. In the past uninformed people, particularly Navajo families, used uranium slag in the foundations and walls of their homes. Over the years, they developed cancer at a rate several times higher than that of the general population.

During its shipment to nuclear power plants, the enriched uranium poses two other dangers: an accident en route, with potential adverse impacts on a local population, and theft by criminals or seizure by terrorists for resale or for nuclear blackmail utilizing homemade atomic bombs that would threaten the lives of urban or regional populations.

Once in the nuclear power plant, the radioactive uranium becomes a very expensive way to boil water as a very inefficient fuel (see Barry Commoner's book, *The Poverty of Power,* for an explanation and evaluation of the process). Its radioactive heat is used to create steam and turn a steam turbine to produce electricity. (This is what was going on at Three Mile Island when the near-catastrophic accident took place.) During this energy production phase of the nuclear fuel cycle, the greatest dangers exist to public health and safety. If the cooling system were to stop working (as at Three Mile Island) there would be a meltdown through the reactor base into the earth (the "China syndrome") and an explosion of steam (a situation barely avoided at Three Mile Island). Since a nuclear reactor contains approximately the radiation of one thousand Hiroshima bombs, there would be a tremendous health hazard posed for people living near the plant or in the path of wind currents carrying radioactive gas and particles. Nuclear plants sited near cities pose not only that threat but also another: in time of war, an enemy need only hit the reactor with a conventional bomb or missile to produce the same effect as a nuclear weapon (a well-placed terrorist explosive could have the same impact). After the Three Mile Island partial meltdown, some of the radiation effects were felt in the few months immediately after the event, while others will take years to be noticed: following the accident, infant mortality rates in the immediate vicinity of the reactor rose four hundred percent, in the state of Pennsylvania rose forty percent, and in areas along the wind current paths rose fifty-two percent outside New York City and twenty-six percent in Maryland. Owners of dairy cattle reported miscarriages at an extremely high rate in the area. And people in the region were subjected to doses of radiation whose impact will emerge as cancers in fifteen to twenty years. (For a scientifically developed, readable analysis of the impacts of Three Mile Island, consult radiologist Dr. Ernest Sternglass' book: *Secret Fallout,* McGraw-Hill, 1981.) Even when a plant is operating "normally" some who work in it are exposed to hazardous levels of radiation, particularly the "jumpers" who do routine or extraordinary repairs on plant components.

The final part of the nuclear fuel cycle is the disposal of radioactive waste. The uranium fuel, in the form of rods, is taken from the core of the reactor when its generating capacity is expended. The rods still contain the hazardous radioactive elements iodine 131, strontium 90, cesium 137 and plutonium. Of these, plutonium, which does not exist naturally, is the most dangerous: one pound of it, if it could be globally distributed, could kill every person on earth; ten pounds of it concentrated in one place could cause a spontaneous nuclear explosion; and it has a half-life of some twenty-four thousand, four hundred years (iodine 131 has a half-life of eight days, strontium 90 of twenty-eight years and cesium 137 of thirty-three years). A half-life means the time it takes for one-half of an element to decay, so it would take half a million years for the plutonium to lose its radioactivity (and a few weeks for iodine, and a few centuries for strontium and cesium). Plutonium is so strong and dangerous, in fact, that if someone were to absorb the minutest particle, die from it and be cremated, the plutonium could be carried by the wind into someone else's lungs and kill again—and so on, for five hundred thousand years. While this highly toxic residue of nuclear power is produced, there is diminishing storage space for it. An interesting moral question is then posed for nuclear fuel advocates: If they would not want the wastes to be dumped in their own backyard, what right have they to impose its dumping in others' backyards?

The nuclear industry, of course, denies any danger from the nuclear fuel cycle. Sometimes it apparently goes to great lengths to suppress adverse publicity: many people believe that Karen Silkwood, a laboratory technician at a Kerr-McGee nuclear plant in Oklahoma, was murdered while on her way to present evidence of nuclear plant hazards to a union representative and a *New York Times* reporter. Silkwood, who was herself dying from plutonium poisoning resulting from her work, died in a mysterious traffic accident on a lonely road—and the evidence she carried with her disappeared. (The movie "The China Syndrome" is based in part on her life.) But denials cannot erase the hazards of a process that contaminates the land.

There is another aspect of the nuclear cycle that is potentially the most dangerous of all: the manufacture of nuclear weapons that utilize the plutonium waste from the nuclear power plants. In them, the ultimate irony of the nuclear cycle is epitomized: an element extracted from the earth has the capability to utterly destroy the earth. Nuclear weapons represent the final contamination of the land: their use would radioactivate and contaminate not just a local area or region but the entire world.

In all of the approaches and occurrences that we have seen thus far, the land is being abused. Alternative perspectives and practices are available, however, and are characteristic of some people of the land. Such people nurture the land and view it as their trust.

NURTURED LAND

In his highly acclaimed book, *The Unsettling of America: Culture and Agriculture*, writer/farmer Wendell Berry discusses two radically different approaches to land use. One approach is that of the *exploiter* (who generally would practice, from our perspective, one or several of the categories of abuse of the land just cited); the other is that of the *nurturer:*

> Let me outline as briefly as I can what seem to me to be the characteristics of these opposite kinds of mind. I conceive a strip-miner to be a model exploiter, and as a model nurturer I take the old-fashioned idea or ideal of a farmer. The exploiter is a specialist, an expert, the nurturer is not. The exploiter's goal is money, profit; the nurturer's goal is health— his land's health, his own, his family's, his community's, his country's. Whereas the exploiter asks of a piece of land only how much and how quickly it can be made to produce, the nurturer asks a question that is much more complex and difficult: what is its carrying capacity? (That is: How much can be taken from it without diminishing it? What can it produce *dependably* for an indefinite time?) The exploiter wishes to earn as much as possible by as little work as possible; the nurturer expects, certainly, to have a decent living from his work, but his characteristic wish is to work *as well* as possible. The competence of the exploiter is in organization; that of the nurturer is in order—a human order, that is, that accommodates itself both to other order and to mystery. The exploiter typically serves an institution or organization; the nurturer serves land, household, community, place. The exploiter thinks in terms of numbers, quantities, "hard facts"; the nurturer in terms of character, condition,

quality, kind. The exploitive always involves the abuse or the perversion of nature and ultimately its destruction. . . .

It is the tragedy of rural America that today the exploitive mind holds sway over the land.

We have described already the effects of the economic and political power exercised by the exploiter. We can see daily, if we look about us, or at the evening news, or in the newspapers, how the earth's air, land, and water resources are being regionally depleted and globally polluted.

The exploiters are not only the landowners or managers or workers. We have all fallen prey, as a people, to the notions that "bigger is better," that machinery is better than human labor in any place or occupation where machinery can be developed to displace labor, that the measure of persons is their material possessions, that people should have an unrestricted right to extend and use their property in whatever manner they choose. With regard to the land and land ownership we are usually far from the perspective of Berry, who writes:

> The true measure of agriculture is not the sophistication of its equipment, the size of its income, or even the statistics of its productivity, but the good health of the land. . . .

And he adds:

> As many as possible should share in the ownership of the land and thus be bound to it by economic interest, by the investment of love and work, by family loyalty, by memory and tradition.

When people are not bound to the land by such ties, when they do not plant their individual and familial roots deep into the soil, they stand over against the earth. Instead of working in harmony with the earth they struggle to dominate the earth.

The *Des Moines Register* editorialized about land use in November 1980 with words that summarize Berry's distinction between nurturers and exploiters and leave us food for thought:

> The issue in land use planning is whether this state's most precious resource—its land—is to be put to its best and proper use for the benefit of future generations or whether natural areas and the state's richest soil is to be exploited to make the biggest buck—and hang the consequences.

At heart is whether we see the earth as a resource to be exploited or as a sustainer of life entrusted to our care.

ENTRUSTED LAND

As we become daily more aware of problems of land ownership and use, we might wonder: "How did we arrive at where we are?" and "Is there an alternative to the danger we face of a world in which a handful of owners control exploited land?"

One of the fundamental changes we have to make if we are to avert the danger of consolidated, exploited land is to treat the earth as a trust from God, good *in itself* (as are all God's works) and good *for us*, for all of us present and future generations. At times in our Western history we have developed an ideological basis for our exploitation of the earth— even to the extent of attempting a biblical justification for it. As we explore ways of restoring and conserving the earth, part of our task must be to reflect on our religious traditions and transform them on the theoretical and practical levels. We must change from an ideology of *dominance of* the land to a God-centered sense of *relation to* the land; we must change from the practice of *exploitation* of the land to the practice of *nurture* of the land. As we engage in this double transformation, we should look to the best of our religioethical heritage for a new vision, a new way of seeing things and a formulation of ways to make the hoped-for future our new present.

We who live in the United States have two rich traditions

upon which we might draw as we formulate our land ethic: the Judaeo-Christian tradition from which most of us emerge who came to this land, and the American Indian tradition from which indigenous peoples emerge. Through an appropriation of the insights of both traditions, we will be able to understand better the earth, what should be our relationship to it and how the way we relate to it indicates how we understand and fulfill our responsibilities as God's stewards on it.

chapter two

Mother Earth and God's Earth

* * *

All living creatures depend on the earth to provide them with the land, water and air they need to exist. Without these resources we could not eat, drink or breathe. Throughout the ages people have realized the importance of this gift of the earth. In some societies the earth has been seen as God's gift to humanity. In others it has been seen as a sacred mother-provider, as "Mother Earth." In our own culture we might see the earth as God's gift to us—but we also refer to "Mother Nature," thus minimally acknowledging that our dependence on the earth makes us in some way children of the earth.

For many Americans today, this understanding of our dependence on the earth has been lost. Most of us live in cities or suburbs. We see our food only as pre-packaged items on supermarket shelves. We do not think about an ear of corn as a seed planted in the earth, watered by rain or an irrigation system, caressed by a prairie breeze, and harvested by a farmer. We might compare the prices of "name brands" and "store brands," but we do not think much beyond that when we purchase food.

Our understanding of the earth's importance as a provider of life would be deepened were we to reflect for a while on American Indian and Judaeo-Christian ways of seeing the land.

The different Indian nations had distinct beliefs and cultic practices. However, there were some views that were shared by all or most Native Americans when the first white explorers

41

from Europe landed on "New World" beaches. And, because over the past century the outright murder of Indians or their deprivation of the necessities of life diminished their numbers, and because during that same period their cultures were deliberately erased when possible, a gradual melding of Indian beliefs led to an even greater similarity in Indian religious perspectives.

Two basic land principles may be seen in indigenous peoples' religious beliefs about Mother Earth. First, people cannot own the land; second, people must treat the land with respect. (It should be noted here that "the land" is a generic term for traditional American Indians. It means, for most, a unity of land, water, and air and, for some, all life forms as well.)

THE LAND CANNOT BE OWNED

When the European settlers arrived on America's coasts, and later when they moved westward, they noticed what was for them a strange phenomenon: native peoples had no concept of buying and selling land. Indian-controlled lands had no fences that separated one family's "property" or one nation's "homeland" from another's. The land was seen as the domain of everyone.

It was true that when a group stayed for a time at a given place a particular spot might be used exclusively by members of a family. But no proprietary claim was intended; family members were merely using a piece of land for a brief moment of time. It was also true that among the different peoples there were territorial rights, over which battles would sometimes be fought. But even these territories were loosely defined, having neither boundary markers to delineate them nor military outposts to defend them. The earth was seen as boundary-less and limitless.

The Indian practice of non-ownership of the land is attested to by speeches Indians gave when offered money or goods for their lands. The Indians did not want to leave their lands, but expanding settlers and the U.S. Cavalry left them no choice. Consider, for example, these words of Chief Joseph of the Nez Perce:

> The country was made without lines of demarcation, and it is no man's business to divide it. . . . I never said the land was mine to do with as I chose. The one who has the right to dispose of it is the one who has created it. (Quoted in T. C. McLuhan's Indian anthology, *Touch the Earth*.)

Tecumseh, the Shawnee chief, spoke in a similar vein. He urged

> . . . all the Redmen to unite in claiming a common and equal right in the land, as it was at first and should be yet; for it was never divided, but belongs to all for the use of each. That no part has a right to sell, even to each other, much less to strangers—those who want all and will not do with less. (Quoted in *Touch the Earth*.)

An unnamed chief of the Blackfeet declared:

> As long as the sun shines and the waters flow, this land will be here to give life to men and animals. We cannot sell the lives of men and animals; therefore we cannot sell this land. It was put here for us by the Great Spirit and we cannot sell it because it does not belong to us. (Quoted in *Touch the Earth*.)

In fact, Indian spirituality saw deeper than mere ownership. The Indian was an integral part of the land. According to the Lakota (Sioux) chief Luther Standing Bear:

> The American Indian is of the soil, whether it be the region of forests, plains, pueblos, or mesas. He fits into the landscape, for the hand that fashioned the continent also fashioned the man for his surroundings. He once grew as naturally as the wild sunflowers; he belongs just as the buffalo belonged. (From *Land of the Spotted Eagle*.)

One cannot own that of which one is a part. The Indian is a part of the land. His relationship to it is deeper and more enduring than the property relationship that exists between other people and the land.

The words of the Lakota holy man, Lame Deer, reinforce the property-less perspective of Native Americans:

> Land does not belong to any single man but to all people and to the future generations. (From *Lame Deer, Seeker of Visions,* by John (Fire) Lame Deer and Richard Erdoes.)

When we relate this thought to that of the previous Indians cited, we might draw several conclusions about the Indian's traditional non-conceptualization of a property relationship that binds some people to a particular part of the land while excluding others from that same part.

Mother Earth is seen as a unity. The land has no dividing lines; it is "made without lines of demarcation." That is its *natural state;* the Great Spirit created it thus. Therefore, to divide the land is to *go against nature,* and hence to go against the Great Spirit. Only the Great Spirit who created the earth and established its harmonies can "dispose of it." No one else can presume that right and power; one cannot exercise a proprietary relationship over what rightfully belongs to another. Therefore, since the earth rightfully belongs to its Creator, people cannot appropriate for themselves the Great Spirit's property. So, two basic principles have been established: the earth is *naturally undivided* and only the Great Spirit can divide it; the earth as the creation of the Great Spirit *belongs to the Great Spirit* and cannot be disposed of by anyone else.

The land that belongs to the Great Spirit has been apportioned in a general way among the nations of the earth for their use. The Red nations, for example, have been given what is now known as the Americas. They were still willing to share what personal property and skills they had with the first white colonists. They allowed those early settlers to cultivate land for their sustenance, without intending that members of the white race should continually expand while erecting exclusionary

fences. The land, after all, "belongs to all for the use of each."
No individual Red nation can sell any part of the land—not
even to another Red nation, much less to whites who "want all
and will not do with less." Other basic principles are established: the land *belongs to all the nations* in a general sense;
part of that "all" *cannot sell the land* to another part (an attitude distinct from the relations among Western nations where
a territory or smaller part of the earth might be transferred by
treaty from one nation to another).

If a nation cannot sell part of what belongs to all, neither
can an individual who is just one part of the nation. The land
belongs to the entire nation, and no individual or family, no
part of the whole, can appropriate for itself a part of the land
nor sell it to another part. Other goods such as those made or
gathered by people could be sold or traded—but not the land.
Not all property was held in common or used in common. But
the land, a non-property, was held in common.

The idea of property was well understood and accepted by
Native Americans. For example, a family or an individual
might own a tepee for shelter, a horse and bow and arrow for
hunting, pottery for cooking and serving food, or clothing for
warmth. Such property could be given as a gift or traded. But
the understanding of property was never extended to the land.
It was inconceivable for the Indians that the land, which was
created by the Great Spirit and which provided for all their
needs, could ever be anyone's property. This same understanding was transferred to other living creatures. For example, the
buffalo could not be bought and sold. The vast herds were
meant for all to provide food, clothing, and shelter. (Hence the
Indians' initial surprise at livestock herds. The Indians did
learn from the Spaniards that horses were meant to be kept in
herds for future use. But this was a later development, and
perhaps an apparent double standard was avoided by seeing
the horse as not a part of the original heritage of the Indian,
and as having less vital a role to play in meeting the Indian's
basic needs.) Once a buffalo was killed, the products made
from it such as dried meat or robes might be traded, but the
living buffalo could not be traded. The buffalo and other living

creatures could never be sold: the nature of life itself made such a practice impossible, for one cannot buy and sell life. (Such an attitude, of course, was directly contrary to the practice of slavery accepted by Europeans and American colonists alike.) Thus, the living Mother Earth cannot be bought and sold. The land was put here for the Indians but, paradoxically for the whites, the Indians cannot buy and sell it "because it does not belong to us."

The Indian, as "part of the soil," is uniquely related to Mother Earth throughout the continent. Paradoxically again, the Indian both puts roots in the soil and is also the soil itself. The roots were loosely planted by many of the Indian nations of the time, who were nomadic. But since they were of the earth no matter where they stopped, even for a brief moment of time, they could become anew a part of the earth, or relate anew to a different part of the earth. They could grow "as naturally as the wild sunflowers" wherever they roamed.

Neither an individual nor a nation in any historical period can own Mother Earth or any part of her. The land belongs "to all people and to the future generations." Thus, non-ownership of the land is ongoing: in the future no individual or nation can divide and appropriate the earth. Every future becomes a new present having its own future. At no point might people of a given present apportion the land and so inhibit its being able to be shared by future generations. The land belongs to everyone now and in the future.

This understanding of the earth as *provider* rather than as *property* is closely related to the second basic American Indian attitude toward the land: people must live in harmony with the earth.

THE LAND MUST BE RESPECTED

Traditional Native Americans regarded the land as the immediate source of life (the Great Spirit was the ultimate source). Just as a human mother provides nourishment for her children and cares for them, Mother Earth provides for her children's needs. She provides fruits and vegetables in their seasons. She provides grassland for the buffalo and forests for the deer so that they might have food and shelter. Directly and indirectly, through her produce and through the animals that graze on her, Mother Earth feeds all of her children.

American Indians had a profound sense of the interrelatedness of all creatures, a sense expressed on occasions when the sacred pipe was smoked:

> The smoke of our sacred pipe is the breath of the Great Spirit. Sitting together smoking the pipe, we form the circle without end, which contains within it every living thing upon this earth. (From *Lame Deer.*)

The Sioux Indians end their important ceremonies with the words "all my relatives," because "all my relatives—plants, animals, humans [are] all one big universal family" (from *Lame Deer*). Thus, people must live in harmony with the earth. The Indian believes that we must "see ourselves as part of this earth, not as an enemy from the outside who tries to impose his will on it" (from *Lame Deer*). This perception disallows abuse of the earth. In the same way that the living Mother Earth cannot be bought and sold, neither can she be harmed. She is both provider of life and extension of life. The Sioux Medicine Man Black Elk speaks of a time when "we were happy in our own country and we were seldom hungry, for then the two-leggeds and the four-leggeds lived together like relatives, and there was plenty for them and for us. . ." (from John G. Neihardt's *Black Elk Speaks*).

Although some Indians did cultivate the land, members of some nomadic nations looked upon farming and mining practices as desecration of the earth. Thus, the holy man Smohalla of the Sokulks in Washington state declared:

> You ask me to plow the ground. Shall I take a knife and tear my mother's breast? Then when I die she will not take me to her bosom to rest. You ask me to dig for stone. Shall I dig under her skin for her bones? Then when I die I cannot en-

ter her body to be born again. You ask me to cut grass and make hay and sell it and be rich like white men. But how dare I cut off my mother's hair? (From *Touch the Earth.*)

This profound sense of a deep filial tie with the earth led some Indians to reject the white society because of the way whites mistreated the earth and her creatures. Black Elk deplored the senseless killing of the buffalo by whites:

I can remember when the bison were so many that they could not be counted, but more and more Wasichu came to kill them until there were only heaps of bones scattered where they used to be. The Wasichu did not kill them to eat: they killed them for the metal that makes them crazy [gold], and they took only the hides to sell. Sometimes they did not even take the hides, only the tongues. ... Sometimes they did not even take the tongues; they just killed and killed because they liked to do that. When we hunted bison, we killed only what we needed. (From *Touch the Earth.*)

The Indians tried to live in harmony with the land, and resented the whites who came in as strangers having no sense of harmony with the earth. According to Chief Luther Standing Bear:

The white man does not understand the Indian for the reason that he does not understand America. He is too far removed from its formative processes. The roots of his tree of life have not yet grasped the rock and soil. The white man is still troubled with primitive fears. ... The man from Europe is still a foreigner and an alien. ... But in the Indian the spirit of the land is still vested; it will be until other men are able to divine and meet its rhythm. Men must be born and reborn to belong. Their bodies must be formed of the dust of their forefathers' bones.

We do not think of the great open plains, the beautiful rolling hills, and winding streams with tangled growth, as "wild." Only to the white man was nature a "wilderness"

and only to him was the land "infested" with "wild" animals
and "savage" people. To us it was tame. Earth was bountiful
and we were surrounded with the blessings of the Great
Mystery. Not until the hairy man from the east came and
with brutal frenzy heaped injustices upon us and the families we loved was it "wild" for us. When the very animals of
the forest began fleeing from his approach, then it was for
us the "Wild West" began. (From *Touch the Earth*.)

For Luther Standing Bear there was a naturally balanced relationship among all life forms. The Indian was one of many
creatures sustained by Mother Earth, living in harmony with
her:

The old life was attuned to nature's rhythm—bound in mys-
tical ties to the sun, moon, and stars; to the waving grasses,
flowing streams and whispering winds. (From *Land of the
Spotted Eagle*.)

The sense of living in harmony with the earth was tied to a
love of the earth and a sense of kinship with other creatures:

The Lakota was a true naturalist—a lover of Nature. He
loved the earth, and all things of the earth, the attachment
growing with age. . . .

The land was loved:

Wherever the Lakota went, he was with Mother Earth. No
matter where he roamed by day or slept by night, he was
safe with her. This thought comforted and sustained the Lakota and he was eternally filled with gratitude. . . .

Animals, birds and fish were seen as relatives:

Kinship with all creatures of the earth, sky, and water was a
real and active principle. For the animal and bird world
there existed a brotherly feeling that kept the Lakota safe
among them. . . .

Some of these animal relatives provided food for people, but their gift of life was never abused:

> The animal had rights—the right of man's protection, the right to live, the right to multiply, the right to freedom, and the right to man's indebtedness—and in recognition of these rights the Lakota never enslaved the animal, and spared all life that was not needed for food and clothing. . . .

People were not seen as being *over* other living creatures, but as *sharers* with them of God's spirit:

> The Lakota could despise no creature, for all were of one blood, made by the same hand, and filled with the essence of the Great Mystery. . . .

Luther Standing Bear concludes:

> The Indian and the white man sense things differently because the white man has put distance between himself and nature; and assuming a lofty place in the scheme of order of things has lost for him both reverence and understanding. . . . And here I find the great distinction between the faith of the Indian and the white man. Indian faith sought the harmony of man with his surroundings; the other sought the dominance of surroundings. . . . For one man the world was full of beauty; for the other it was a place of sin and ugliness to be endured until he went to another world. . . . (From *Land of the Spotted Eagle.*)

The traditional American Indian, then, felt close to the earth and other living beings. The earth was not to be conquered, for it was not harmful or threatening but family; it was to be treated with respect. That Indian perspective, according to Luther Standing Bear, sharply contrasts with the white person's perspective.

One cannot romanticize the Indians, for to do so would deprive them of life. Today the perspective of the traditional American Indian is not shared by the majority of his or her nation; it is a minority view. Thus, there are Indians who exploit the earth and their own people for monetary gain:

> Among our own now, when a person attains a little power, he also turns into an exploiter and an intimidator. This can be profitable; therefore many Indians have sought leadership with this very end in mind. (From Thomas E. Mails, *Fools Crow.*)

But the basic tradition persists, and is passed on by the elders to those who will accept it—much as Christianity is lived by the few who are willing to follow in Jesus' footsteps.

Is Luther Standing Bear correct in his interpretation of the two faiths, Indian and Christian? In some ways, yes. But in other ways, perhaps it might be more accurate to call the two faiths that Standing Bear describes Indian and *white*—because although the phrase "subdue the earth" is part of the Judaeo-Christian tradition, in its biblical context it is not meant to imply the abuse of the earth that is characteristic of "Christian" industrial societies. In fact, in the Judaeo-Christian tradition there are found perspectives parallel to those of the American Indian: the earth is God's, and is meant to be shared by God's creatures; the earth must be cared for.

THE LAND IS GOD'S

In the Book of Genesis we read the beautiful creation story and learn two fundamental truths: everything in the universe has been created by God; everything that God creates is good:

> In the beginning God created the heavens and the earth. . . . God said "Let there be light"; and there was light. And God saw that the light was good. . . . And God said, "Let there be a firmament in the midst of the waters. . . ." And it was so. . . . And God said, "Let the waters under the heavens be gathered together into one place, and let the dry land ap-

pear." And it was so. . . . And God saw that it was good. And God said, "Let the earth put forth vegetation. . . ." And it was so. . . . And God saw that it was good. . . . And God said, "Let there be lights in the firmament of the heavens to separate the day from the night. . . ." And it was so. . . . And God saw that it was good. . . . And God said, "Let the waters bring forth swarms of living creatures, and let birds fly above the earth. . . ." And God saw that it was good. . . . And God said, "Let the earth bring forth living creatures according to their kinds: cattle and creeping things and beasts of the earth. . . ." And God saw that it was good. . . . Then God said, "Let us make man in our image, after our likeness, and let them have dominion over the fish of the sea, and over the birds of the air, and over the cattle, and over every creeping thing that creeps over the earth." So God created man in his own image, in the image of God he created him: male and female he created them. And God said to them, "Be fruitful and multiply, and fill the earth and subdue it; and have dominion over the fish of the sea and over the birds of the air and over every living thing that moves upon the earth. . . ." And God saw everything that he had made, and behold, it was very good. . . (Genesis 1:1–31).

God set the man over all the other creatures (the understanding of the time was that to name something implies power over it and superiority to it; thus, for example, God changed Abram's name to Abraham, but the Jews never pronounced God's name):

The man gave names to all cattle, and to the birds of the air, and to every beast of the field. . . (Genesis 2:20).

The writers of the Old Testament try to show that everything in the universe that we see or hear or otherwise learn about flows from the creative love of God: time, the seasons, the climate, air, land, water, celestial bodies, and the life that flies, swims, walks, or crawls. People, who are made in God's image, are given charge of the rest of creation. God's ownership of the land exists, then, because God has created it and has dominion over it.

God's ultimate ownership of the land is taught throughout the Bible. In the Book of Psalms, for example, we read:

> The Lord's are the earth and its fullness;
> the world and those who dwell in it (Psalm 24:1).

In Sirach (42:15–43) God's creative power and presence in nature are poetically described with such comments as:

> How beautiful are all his works!
> even to the spark and fleeting vision!
> The universe abides and lives forever,
> to meet each need each creature is preserved.
> Let the last word be:
> he is all in all (42:23–24; 43:28).

And the psalmist exclaims:

> O Lord, our Lord,
> how glorious is your name over all the earth!
> When I behold your heavens, the work of your fingers,
> the moon and the stars which you set in place—
> what is man that you should be mindful of him,
> or the son of man that you should care for him? (8:2, 4–5).

The sovereignty of God is proclaimed; humanity is humbled before God's power and majesty; dominion over the earth is ultimately God's prerogative.

In the Book of Leviticus, God tells the Jewish people:

> The land belongs to me and to me you are only strangers
> and guests (25:23).

We are "strangers and guests" on God's land; we are not true property owners. We have charge of a portion of the earth, for a brief moment in time and human history, in a particular place, according to the civil laws of the particular political entity or entities by whom our civic lives are governed. St. Thomas Aquinas points out in the *Summa Theologica* that the natural law, a reflection of the eternal law of God, teaches the community of possessions. We might say by extension that the earth is indivisible, and that its fruits are meant for all. St. Thomas declares that human laws of property have been devised to promote stability in society. The division of possessions is based on *positive law* (law devised by people living in society) rather than on *natural law* (law inherent in rational beings that inclines them to their proper act and end as participants in the *eternal law* of God to which everything is subject):

> Community of goods is ascribed to the natural law, not that the natural law dictates that all things should be possessed in common and that nothing should be possessed as one's own: but because the division of possessions is not according to the natural law, but rather arose from human agreement which belongs to positive law, as stated above (Q. 57, art. 2–3). Hence the ownership of possessions is not contrary to the natural law, but an addition thereto devised by human reason (Q. 66, art. 2).

"Human reason" made this addition because "every man is more careful to procure what is for himself alone than that which is common to many or to all," because "human affairs are conducted in more orderly fashion if each man is charged with taking care of some particular thing himself," and because "a more peaceful state is ensured to man if each one is contented with his own." St. Thomas adds that, with respect to the use of property, "man ought to possess external things, not as his own, but as common, so that, to wit, he is ready to communicate them to others in their need." If people do not fulfill their responsibility of sharing goods, then in extreme necessity people are allowed to take from those who have an abundance of goods in order to satisfy their own or their neighbor's need:

> In cases of need all things are common property, so that there would seem to be no sin in taking another's property, for need has made it common (Q. 66, art. 7).

St. Thomas concludes, first, that "it is not theft, properly speaking, to take secretly and use another's property in extreme need: because that which he takes for the support of his life becomes his own property by reason of that need"; and second, that "in a case of a like need a man may also take secretly another's property in order to succor his neighbor in need" (Q. 66, art. 17).

This attitude toward property is seen with regard to the land and its fruits in Deuteronomy, where the hungry person is allowed to partake of produce on another's land:

> When you go through your neighbor's vineyard, you may eat as many of his grapes as you wish, but do not put them in your basket. When you go through your neighbor's grainfield, you may pluck some of the ears with your hand, but do not put a sickle to your neighbor's grain. (23:25–26).

The civil right to the land and its fruits, then, is not absolute: the land is God's, and through God's goodness it provides for the needs of all of God's creatures. It would follow, then, that because "God created humanity in God's image, in the divine image God created them, male and female God created them" (Genesis 1:27) we should care for the earth with the same solicitude for others with which God created it: everything that God created is *good,* and the earth has been given the ability to continually express God's goodness by *providing for the needs* of all living creatures. Because we are made in God's image and likeness, we have been given a special trust during our tenure on the land. We have been given charge of the earth and are God's vicarious owners—but only to the extent that we, like God, create what is good and work with the earth to meet the needs of the earth's creatures. We have been chosen to image God in our attitude toward, and practices upon, the earth. We are called to be God's stewards upon the land.

PEOPLE ARE GOD'S STEWARDS ON THE LAND

We have seen earlier how the creation story in Genesis 1 teaches that God created the world and all in it, and that everything that God creates is good. God then gave to "the man" (humanity) *dominion* over the rest of creation, and this authority of dominion was reinforced in the story of Adam naming all the animals.

Part of humanity's *responsibility* for the earth also is described in Genesis. Adam is presented as the gardener in Eden:

> The Lord God then took the man and settled him in the garden of Eden, to cultivate and care for it (2:15).

This verse might seem to contradict the verses previously mentioned (Genesis 1:26, 28) where humanity is told to have "dominion" over the rest of creation and to "subdue" the earth. But we might actually see here the nature of subduing and the fullness of dominion.

SUBDUING THE EARTH

The earth is "subdued" when people work with it to meet their needs. For example, through cultivation of the land people convert part of the earth to agriculture from its untouched state. The ordered beauty of the farm replaces the pristine beauty of untouched land. The farmer, who is a part of nature, re-forms the land to serve humanity, which is also part of nature. The farmer tends the land in the spirit of Adam: the garden of Eden is now every farmer's land. We speak at times of fertile agricultural land as a "garden spot." On a large scale, then, farmers tend their gardens in fulfillment of their responsibilities toward God, whose stewards they are.

The meaning of "cultivation" should be extended beyond the confines of agriculture. We cultivate the earth also through responsible forestry and mining practices.

We sometimes think of agriculture or other ways of working the land as changing "nature." Thus, we might speak of "natural beauty," meaning that people have not yet altered the earth in a particular place. But, as we have noted, we, too, are part of "nature." We share with all of the universe a common origin: God's creative love. True, *we* are created in God's image and likeness, but we are *created* in God's image and likeness. And so, *as part of creation* we are given responsibility for the rest of creation.

The implication of this is that we are not rendering an area "unnatural" just by virtue of changing it. If we work *with* the earth we are ordering nature in a different way, but are still dependent on the earth to meet our needs. We who love the earth should not regard *all* alterations of the earth, then, with a blanket sense of dismay. Rather, we should understand that we have a role to play in aiding the earth to meet our human needs. In that respect we image God who formed the earth and the natural laws that govern it in such a way that it could provide for the needs of all living creatures.

Our reaction against land alteration, of course, is based on the reality that people do abuse the earth terribly. We poison the air with industrial smoke, automobile emissions, acid rain, and radioactive gas. We poison the water with industrial wastes, urban sewage, high phosphate detergents and agricultural herbicides, pesticides, and fertilizers. We poison the land with wastes: industrial waste dumping, nuclear waste "storage," agricultural chemical inputs. We divert agricultural water for industrial and recreational uses. We remove the best agricultural land from production by building suburbs, shopping malls, airports and highways on it, or by stripmining it and leaving it scarred and barren. We imbed in the earth in storage silos nuclear missiles that have the capacity to render the whole earth a wasteland.

For some people, therefore, the earth is beautiful only where humanity has not altered it. We do not understand the meaning of land stewardship—nor are we realistic about satisfying human hunger, for an untilled earth could not provide all of our needs. We have not yet accepted our role in and responsibility for the created world; we have lost the sense of being rooted in nature.

Our understanding of stewardship does not mean, however, that wherever we wish we might alter the earth, even if that alteration is done slowly and gently. We still need areas of pristine beauty. We need places where we might see how the earth's rhythms and harmonies flow: the passage of the seasons, the interaction among life forms, the birth to death cycle of other creatures. In such places we can appreciate the earth's regenerative power, and so better appreciate not only its beauty and harmony but also the loving genius of its Creator.

Our stewardship of the earth means, then, that we must both work with the earth and let the earth live undisturbed. In both instances, we are part of the earth's rhythm and harmony.

We must also be conscious, when we work with the earth, that we are striving to meet human *needs* and not human *wants*. Human needs are basic and finite. Human wants are superfluous and infinite. It is difficult at times to distinguish between them, because we need not just food, clothing and shelter but also physical, social, and spiritual well-being, and the degree of need varies from person to person. For example, children might need more food than the elderly, but the elderly might need warmer homes during the cold winter months. Or all of us depend on energy of one type or another to supply our home and factory needs, but different climates determine the amount necessary for us. It is our particular problem in the middle and upper classes of the United States that we have come to identify our wants with our needs and try to rationalize the absurdity of superfluities on the grounds of "psychological need." And while we are caught up in consumerism, others in our country and throughout the world are desperately trying to survive on what we have left them of the earth's land, water, and mineral resources.

What we must learn anew is to "subdue" the earth rather than to "subjugate" the earth. We must carefully cultivate it rather than callously corrupt it.

HAVING DOMINION OVER THE EARTH

As God's stewards, we are responsible for relating to the land in the way that God relates to it. If we are to image God's loving solicitude for creation, then we must care for the earth and its creatures. When we exercise dominion over the rest of creation, we are acting as God's caretakers on the earth.

When God entrusted the garden of Eden to Adam (Genesis 2:15), God entrusted all of the earth to humanity's care. Adam's reception of the responsibility of caring for the earth represents our reception of the same responsibility as Adam's descendants.

Stewardship as caring means that we have been charged for a time (during our personal and communal history) with working with that part of the earth conferred on us by local, national, or international law. It means that we are responsible for the way we use the land that is under our individual or corporate control. It means that we are responsible for the care with which that land is treated. Thus, our dominion over the earth means that, as God's stewards, we are the land's *custodians* and *conservers.* We have custody of the land according to whatever property laws are extant during the time when, and in the place where, we as individuals or as members of a larger community have charge of a part of the earth. We must *conserve* that land so that it will be able to continue yielding its resources in the future. When we are custodians and conservers of the land we are also *co-creators* with God. We work with God, according to the processes that God has placed in the world and the laws that govern those processes, to guide the earth's productivity and conserve its gifts.

Our dominion over the earth confers on us a great responsibility. More than any other creature we have the power to control the earth's destiny. We are able to choose among alternate possibilities for the earth's development. We are able to alter the course of rivers, level mountains, displace vegetation, and render other creatures—and ourselves—extinct. If our dominion over the earth is rightly understood as our exercise of responsible control, on God's behalf, of the land entrusted to our care, we will work *with* the earth as part *of* the earth. In so doing we will be faithful images of God from within creation.

What we must learn is to have *dominion* over the earth rather than to *dominate* the earth. We must respectfully care for the land rather than rapaciously covet it.

MOTHER EARTH AND GOD'S EARTH

We are children of God and of the earth. God has created us and the earth on which we live. The earth provides for our needs: it nourishes us with its produce, refreshes us with its water, and sustains our breath of life with its air. We were formed from it and shall return to become part of it; we are made of it and to it we shall return. God cares for our needs: through the earth God nourishes our bodies; through grace God nourishes our spirits. We were formed by God and destined to be one with God; we are God's images, destined to unite with the One whose reflection we are.

When we who are Christians reflect on the biblical and American Indian religious traditions, we become aware of the ways in which they converge in their perspective on the land. Some fundamental differences exist: the earth is more personalized in the Indian tradition; humanity has a caretaker role in the Judaeo-Christian tradition. But the similarities are greater, and even where differences do exist there is some overlap and, for Christians and traditional Indians, ways in which we might learn from each other—or, at the very least, come to know and respect each other's perspectives as equally being concerned about understanding and living according to the Spirit's loving presence in the world.

Some years ago, Secretary of the Interior Stewart Udall wrote:

> In recent decades we have slowly come back to some of the truths that the Indians knew from the beginning: that unborn generations have a claim on the land equal to our own; that men need to learn from nature, to keep an ear to the earth, and to replenish their spirits in frequent contacts with animals and wild land. And most important of all, we are recovering a sense of reverence for the land. (From *The Quiet Crisis.*)

If we take his suggestion as our starting point as we look at the world about us and reflect on our own and the American Indian's religious traditions, we might begin to recover our Christian tradition from the use to which it has been put in the service of those who have exploited the land. Lynn White, Jr., in his essay "The Historical Roots of Our Ecologic Crisis" (*Science* magazine, March 10, 1967), points out how the biblical perspective of humanity-over-nature provided an ideological foundation for the exploitation of the earth. According to White, what might be extrapolated from Genesis is this:

> Man named all the animals, thus establishing his dominance over them. God planned all of this explicitly for man's benefit and rule: no item in the physical creation had any purpose save to serve man's purposes. And, although man's body is made of clay, he is not simply part of nature; he is made in God's image.

With this as a base, Christianity subsequently

> ... not only established a dualism of man and nature but also insisted that it is God's will that man exploit nature for his proper ends.... By destroying pagan animism [the belief that all natural phenomena possess souls] Christianity made it possible to exploit nature in a mood of indifference to the feelings of natural objects.... We are superior to nature, contemptuous of it, willing to use it for our slightest whim.

White believes that we will not be able to curtail abuses of the earth except by turning away from what he sees as the main Christian perspective:

> Hence we shall continue to have a worsening ecological crisis until we reject the Christian axiom that nature has no reason for existence save to serve man.

For White, an alternative Christian view was that proposed by St. Francis of Assisi, who "tried to substitute the idea of the equality of all creatures, including man, for the idea of man's limitless rule of creation." White laments St. Francis' failure and ends his essay with the proposal that St. Francis be "a patron saint for ecologists."

Although we must dispute some of White's interpretation of the thrust of the Christian understanding of the relation of people to the earth, we must also recognize, nevertheless, that he has pinpointed what has become over the centuries the dominant perspective on the land present in Christianity: we are above nature, and so nature is here to serve us. The perspective of St. Francis, in contrast, is that we are one with nature and must live in harmony with all of God's creation. We can see in St. Francis an attitude that is similar in many ways to that of the American Indian.

How, then, might we reconcile our tradition with the American Indian tradition? Where do they converge and overlap?

OWNING THE LAND

As we have seen, both traditions teach that the earth cannot be regarded as exclusively human property because, ultimately, the land is God's. The Indian might say that "the earth is our sacred Mother; she cannot be owned and divided because she is living and gives life to us all." The Christian might say that "the earth is God's, intended to provide for God's creatures; it is under the care of people acting as God's surrogates and imaging God's concern."

In both traditions we have a sense that we are pilgrims on the land, that our presence here is temporary, that our tenure is limited in time and extent. For the Indian, this might mean that no one can hold title to any land and exercise proprietary rights over it. For the Christian, this might mean that those who hold civil title to a part of the earth might exercise proprietary rights over it for a time in order to meet the needs of their family, their local and national communities, and the world at large. (Christians might also, in the spirit of the Christian community described in chapters 2 and 4 of the Book of

Acts in the New Testament, decide to own land communally.) In both cases, the basic understanding and the net result are the same: the underlying understanding is that the land ultimately is God's; the end result is that the land provides for the needs of *all* of God's children; it does not serve just those who hold civil title to it.

It might be argued that it was easy for Indian peoples to see the earth as boundary-less and indivisible into "property" because of their limited populations on a seemingly limitless land, whereas today we are in a different situation because billions of people inhabit an obviously limited and common land base. However, the latter situation perhaps even more should make us appropriate and adapt for our own time and space the Indian perspective: for if the land is limited, and people need it for their very survival, then what right has an individual, a corporation or a nation to reserve for their exclusive use part of the earth intended by God for all of us? Unlimited land makes fences unnecessary and inconceivable; limited land makes fences untenable and unconscionable. Our consciousness of our planet's limited area and of people's present and future needs should make us reflect carefully on the property question. We must determine if, where and when land as property will benefit the human family. We must be conscious of our obligations to God and to our global brothers and sisters if we do hold land as property.

RESPECTING THE LAND

Just as Christian and American Indian understandings of land ownership converge, the religious perspectives of both groups might conflate in their attitude of respect for the earth.

We have seen how the Indians believe that we are all to live in harmony with the earth. We are to flow with its rhythms and co-exist with its other life forms. We are to take from it and of them only what we need. We have seen also that our Christian tradition teaches us to care for the earth. We are to be God's stewards, responsible for the well-being of an earth entrusted by God to our care. We are to work with that earth to provide for human needs. The Indian might say: "We care for Mother Earth; we are one with her." The Christian might say: "We care for God's earth; we have dominion over it."

In both traditions we understand that we must respect the earth. Whether we see ourselves as part of the earth or caretakers of the earth, we recognize the same fundamental responsibility: to live on the earth in such a way that our presence enhances and conserves it, for the benefit of all life. The end result of this attitude should be that we care for the land and equitably distribute its benefits.

If we who are Christians live according to this theme of our tradition, a new relationship, a non-exploitive one, will come to characterize our pilgrim presence on the earth. No longer would we be accused of justifying—on an ideological level—the ruination—on a practical level—of the land.

Mother Earth and God's earth are one and the same: we live on a single planet. We might view the land from different perspectives, but the same land is seen by all of us, and how we view it will help determine what we do with it. If we look at the earth as sacred or as a sacred trust, we will respect and care for it rather than despise and abuse it. We will realize that we must work in harmony with it rather than in conflict with it. We will share it among ourselves and with our descendants rather than reserve it for a few people now and in the future. We will carefully conserve it so that it will provide for ourselves and future generations rather than be exploited and wasted to satisfy one generation's selfishness.

As children of God and the earth, we must explore ways to promote harmony in creation. We must seek to deepen our understanding of our role as pilgrims and stewards on the land.

chapter three

Pilgrims and Stewards

* * *

We Americans are a remarkably mobile people. The majority of us will move several times during our lives, and probably spend our last days in a city or town far from our birthplace. We are, in a sense, nomads, not in the same way as those who wander from place to place because of diminishing supplies of water or food, but nomads nonetheless. We might travel from place to place seeking a higher paying or more fulfilling job, a better home or a different climate. Sometimes we do so from necessity, just as other nomads did who preceded us; we lose a job or accept a promotion and so must relocate to hold a different position.

The drawback of a nomadic existence is that we might become rootless and never feel part of a place. We might feel as if we are always "in between" our last locale and our future one. In some ways our rootlessness could be harmful to ourselves and to the land. We might become afraid to form bonds of friendship as we travel about, and so feel few ties to each new community in which we live. We might have no sense of the history of a place, no affinity for the particular part of the earth that is our new dwelling place. Our sense of rootlessness represents our alienation from our local human family and from the land on which we live.

In other ways our nomadic existence might be beneficial to us and to the land. We could become aware of our responsibility to create or become part of a community wherever we go, accepting its transitory nature for ourselves. We could strive to care for the land wherever we go and avoid an exclusively proprietary relationship with it. We could realize that the land ultimately belongs to its enduring owner, God, who intended it to serve future wanderers as well as ourselves; and we could realize that wherever we go we can become part of a new part of the earth. Our sense of being nomads or wanderers on the earth can also make us aware of our ultimate destiny: to be united with the One whose image we are.

We are pilgrims on and stewards of the land. We sojourn on earth as pilgrims on a journey and yet, paradoxically, as inhabitors and inheritors of a homeland entrusted by God to our care.

A PILGRIM PEOPLE

In the history of Western civilization, probably the best known example of a nomadic people is the Jews of the Old Testament. The story of their liberation from slavery in Egypt and subsequent forty years of wandering in the Sinai desert are described in the Book of Exodus. The event has had great significance for the Jewish people: it is referred to in other Old Testament writings and influences the politics of the state of Israel today. It is also significant for Christians: it is part of our own religious heritage and influences the political statements (which do not necessarily coincide with political beliefs or commitments) of Christian-majority nations toward Israel.

The Book of Exodus opens with the Jewish people in bondage in Egypt. They had to do forced labor (1:11), then they were reduced to slavery (1:14) and finally, their male babies were put to death at birth (1:16, 22). In order to free the Jews from this oppression God calls Moses to deliver them, telling him:

> I have witnessed the affliction of my people in Egypt and
> have heard their cry of complaint against their slave drivers,
> so I know well what they are suffering. Therefore I have

come down to rescue them from the hands of the Egyptians
and lead them out of that land into a good and spacious
land, a land flowing with milk and honey. . . (3:7–8).

The people are to be delivered from the land of oppression
and led to the land of liberation. The earth which was inhospitable for them in one locus, not because of its natural characteristics but because of the social system governing human
relations on it, was to be hospitable to them in another place,
where God's dominion would be recognized and God's bounty
would be allowed to flow freely from creation. We see here a
reversal of the Genesis story of Adam and Eve being cast out of
the garden of Eden because of their sin. In that narrative, the
land was hospitable to humanity, but became inhospitable
when people abused its gifts and harmony; but in Exodus an
inhospitable land is to be exchanged for an hospitable land. In
Genesis, Adam and Eve are exiled from a land of plenty into a
harsher environment; in Exodus, the Jewish people are called
from exile to a new homeland—one, in fact, where other people already dwell and must be cast out in turn (3:8). The Jews
will be converted from oppressed aliens in a strange land to
triumphant inhabitants of a bountiful homeland.

After their escape from Egypt, made possible by God's
power, the Israelites set out for their promised land. As they
entered the desert the going was rough. They complained
about being brought there by Moses and his brother Aaron,
their leaders, and yearned for their former life in Egypt (16:2–
3). Food was scarce and the Lord intervened miraculously to
provide them with quail and manna (Ch. 16). Water was
scarce, but again God miraculously met their need (17:1–7).
The fruits of the land, and so land itself, became important to a
landless people. The land was to be the physical and social base
in which the people might plant their own roots as well as sow
seed, and so overcome psychological and physical rootlessness
and alienation from the earth. As they wandered in the desert,
though, they became acutely aware of God's power over creation and of God's ultimate ownership of the land. They could

not provide for themselves, for the desert area through which they passed was mostly dry, barren, and unproductive. They could not live in harmony with the land. But God could make the earth satisfy their hunger because God is in harmony with the land.

God's harmony with the earth was manifested when God provided food in seemingly barren places. God's ultimate ownership of the land was emphasized when God promised land to the Israelites if they would keep their covenant (agreement) with God to fulfill God's will:

> You shall be my special possession, dearer to me than all other people, though all the earth is mine (Exodus 19:5).

The earth is God's, and as he led the Israelites through the land, they recognized more fully his sovereignty over it—and over them as well. (During their period of wandering in the desert God gave them, through Moses, the Ten Commandments and other laws and rules of conduct.)

When they came into their new land, the Jews were supposed to treat each other justly, be kind to the stranger among them, and treat the land with care. Through these practices they would live in harmony with each other, with other peoples, and with the earth itself.

One of the ways in which the Israelites were to practice justice toward each other was in the distribution of the land. When they arrived in Canaan and conquered it from other peoples, God instructed them to divide their new land equitably. No individual or family or tribe was to have either an advantage in selecting sites or the right to appropriate extensive amounts of land:

> You shall take possession of the land and settle in it, for I have given you the land as your property. You shall apportion the land among yourselves by lot, clan by clan, assigning a large heritage to a large group and a small heritage to

a small group. Wherever anyone's lot falls, there shall his property be within the heritage of his ancestral tribe (Numbers 33:53–54).

Thus, by a process of casting lots, equivalent today to a chance roll of the dice, people were given the plots of land that were to serve their needs and the needs of their descendants. The land they received was to remain in their family through time. As we shall see later, even if some of them were to lose their land to others, every fifty years they would have the right to regain it.

The sense of justice underlying equitable land distribution also carried over into the way in which land was set aside for towns. Once again the land was to be equitably distributed, or rather, in this case, equitably *re*distributed, as it was converted from agricultural use to urban uses. The land was to be taken from production *proportionally:*

> In assigning the cities from the property of the Israelites, take more from a larger group and fewer from a smaller one, so that each group will cede cities to the Levites in proportion to its own heritage (Numbers 35:8).

The basic principles underlying all land transactions were that the land belongs ultimately to God, that particular families and their descendants were to hold perpetual title to that part of it which had been assigned to them by lot, that they retained title even when their land was lost to others' use, and could regain control of it in the jubilee year, which was to occur every fifty years, and that the land was intended by God to serve the needs of the people as a whole, in the present and the future, and so must be used by them in the best possible way. In the Book of Leviticus God instructs the people about property relations in land through these words:

> Land must not be sold in perpetuity, for the land belongs to me, and to me you are only strangers and guests. You will

allow a right of redemption on all your landed property. If your brother falls on evil days and has to sell his patrimony, his nearest relation shall come to him and exercise his right of redemption on what his brother has sold. . . . In the jubilee year, the [purchaser] must relinquish it and return to his own property (25:23–25, 28).

From God's perspective, we are "strangers and guests" upon *God's* land. This does not mean that we are estranged from the land. As we have seen earlier, God made us stewards of creation, and instructed us to live in harmony with it. We are "strangers and guests" upon the land in that we are pilgrims—nomads—on God's land, that is, we have no ultimate proprietary claim to the land. No individual, no family, no state, no group can claim the land as their own. They might hold civic title to it, or erect artificial national boundaries around it, but they can never really own it; only God owns it. God is telling us that the land is not to be seen as property, as something intended for the exclusive benefit or use of those who have a civil claim to it. People are not to see their relationships to the land in proprietary or economic terms: they are to regard themselves as temporary sojourners and aliens as far as their economic ties to the land are concerned. The land is to be a community benefit, not a private preserve.

If the people live in harmony with the land and with each other, obeying God's commandments, God will bless their labors on the land:

If you live in accordance with my precepts and are careful to observe my commandments, I will give you rain in due season, so that the land will bear its crops, and the trees their fruit; your threshing will last till vintage time, and your vintage till the time for sowing, and you will have food to eat in abundance, so that you may dwell securely in your land (Leviticus 26:3–5).

Their lives will be transformed: in the days of oppression in Egypt, and through the forty years of wandering in the desert, the Israelites found the land to be harsh, and they could not work with it. But now the Lord of creation would guarantee their strength and the earth's fertility. The imagery is once again a reversal of that of Genesis, in which Adam and Eve are cast out from the land of plenty. Here, the people are to be restored to a fertile environment.

In two land-oriented celebrations the Jewish people were to observe God's commands referring to the use and distribution of the land. These were the *sabbatical year* and the *jubilee year*. The sabbatical year was intended to *rejuvenate* the land, and the jubilee year was intended to *redistribute* the land.

THE SABBATICAL YEAR

The practice of the sabbatical year was to have two objectives for the people: to conserve the valuable land base, and to express faith in God. The Jews were told by God:

> When you enter the land that I am giving you, let the land, too, keep a sabbath for the Lord. For six years you may sow your field, and for six years prune your vineyards, gathering in their produce. But during the seventh year the land shall have a complete rest, a sabbath for the Lord, when you may neither sow your field nor prune your vineyard. The aftergrowth of your harvest you shall not reap, nor shall you pick the grapes of your untrimmed vines in this year of sabbath rest for the land (Leviticus 25:2–5).

Every seven years, therefore, the land was to lie fallow. The people were to believe that God would grant them, in the sixth year of their planting, a harvest that would meet their food and seed needs until the time of the harvest in the first year after the sabbatical year. The sixth year's fruits would also have to provide for the feed and foraging needs of their livestock, and of wild animals as well (Leviticus 25:7). The sabbath year reflected the sabbath day, the day of rest and prayerful reflection. Just as God had rested on the seventh day in the creation story (Genesis 2:2–3) and observed the fruits of six days' labor, the Jews were to rest on the seventh day and reflect on what God had made and on their relation to God. The year of rest for the land, in a similar way, was to be a year of rejuvenation for it and for the people, who also were making an act of faith in God and in God's sovereignty over the land, much as they did every week but on a level with immediate practical consequences: the land might or might not be able to satisfy their basic need for food. In faith, they believed that it would, but as the spring planting season came and went without them sowing seed, they must have been somewhat concerned about their survivability. Leviticus addressed this concern, as did Jesus many generations later. In Leviticus the Israelites were told:

> Therefore do not say, "What shall we eat in the seventh year, if we do not then sow or reap our crop?" I will bestow such blessings on you in the sixth year that there will then be crop enough for three years (25:20–21).

Later, Jesus would tell his followers:

> Do not be concerned for your life, what you are to eat, or for your body, what you are to wear. . . . Your Father knows that you need such things (Luke 12:22, 30; cf. Matthew 6:25, 31).

Jesus told them that the God who cares for the birds of the air and the lilies of the field is even more concerned about people's needs, and will provide for them.

One of the petitions in the Lord's Prayer (from the same chapter in Matthew's Gospel) also addressed the sabbatical year (and jubilee year) concern about satisfying hunger:

> Give us this day our daily bread (6:11).

It is a recognition of God's ultimate power over, and concerned involvement in, creation. The God who miraculously gave a hungry, landless people manna in the desert can also provide for hungry people in other contexts. Landless or landed, the people can trust in the Lord to provide for their needs.

The same God who had solicitously freed the Israelites from Egypt and cared for them in the desert also required their obedience. Thus, while the land would yield its fruits to them if they were faithful to their covenant with God, it could also be harsh toward them if they were disobedient:

> But if you do not heed me and do not keep all these commandments, if you reject my precepts and spurn my decrees, refusing to obey all my commandments and breaking my covenant, then I, in turn, will give you your deserts. . . . You will sow your seed in vain, for your enemies will consume the crop. . . . I will make the sky above you as hard as iron, and your soil as hard as bronze, so that your strength will be spent in vain; your land will bear no crops, and its trees no fruit (Leviticus 26:14–17, 19–20).

One of the causes of God's displeasure might be the Israelites' disdain for the sabbatical year; thus God's punishment would cause its prescriptions to be fulfilled so that the land might rest:

> So devastated will I leave the land that your very enemies who come to live there will stand aghast at the sight of it. You yourselves I will scatter among the nations at the point of my drawn sword, leaving your countryside desolate and your cities deserted. Then shall the land retrieve its lost sabbaths during all the time it lies waste, while you are in the land of your enemies; then shall the land have rest and make up for its sabbaths during all the time that it lies desolate, enjoying the rest that you would not let it have on the sabbaths when you lived there (Leviticus 26:32–35).

The land cannot be overworked; to deplete it of its nutrients would be to violate a trust God had given to the Jews. If the people do not allow it to rejuvenate itself, then it will do so when they are scattered far from it.

The sabbatical year, then, was to benefit both the land and the people of the land. The rest from human labor that it demanded would allow the land to regenerate itself, and the people to rededicate themselves to its care and to service to God.

THE JUBILEE YEAR

While the sabbatical year was practiced to prevent the land from being used up by its inhabitants, the jubilee year was practiced to prevent a few among the land's inhabitants from appropriating for themselves the heritage of an entire people. The jubilee year, which was, in effect, a special sabbatical year occurring every seventh sabbatical year (or every fifty years counting the preceding jubilee year), is mandated by God in Leviticus:

> Seven weeks of years shall you count—seven times seven years—so that the seven cycles amount to forty-nine years. Then, on the tenth day of the seventh month let the trumpet resound; on this, the Day of Atonement, the trumpet blast shall re-echo throughout your land. This fiftieth year you shall make sacred by proclaiming liberty in the land for all its inhabitants. It shall be a jubilee for you, when every one of you shall return to his own property, every one to his own family estate. In this fiftieth year, your year of jubilee, you shall not sow, nor shall you reap the aftergrowth or pick the grapes from the untrimmed vines. Since this is the jubilee, which shall be sacred for you, you may not eat of its produce, except as taken directly from the field. In this year of jubilee, then, every one of you shall return to his own property (25:8–13).

The jubilee year had four major components, all of which affected the Israelite economy in a way that was advantageous for the poor and disadvantageous for the rich: the Israelite slaves were to be set free (Leviticus 25:10, 40–43), landed property was to be returned to its original civil owners (Leviticus 25:10, 13, 23–25, 31–34), the soil was to lie fallow, as in the other sabbatical years (Leviticus 25:11–12, 20–22), and all debts were to be forgiven, also as required in the sabbatical year (Deuteronomy 15:1–2; Leviticus 25:39–40). The jubilee year was therefore a time of social transformation, a time of re-establishing God's dominion of justice over the land and its inhabitants.

The proclamation of the jubilee year was not limited to the Old Testament. Jesus also proclaimed the jubilee year to the people of his time. This is apparent in several of his sermons, sayings, and prayers. (For at least one biblical scholar, the proclamation of the jubilee year was a major component of Jesus' ministry: see John Howard Yoder's *The Politics of Jesus.*) Consider, for example, the way in which Jesus opens his ministry in Luke's Gospel, reading from the prophet Isaiah (61:1–2):

> When the book of the prophet Isaiah was handed him, he unrolled the scroll and found the passage where it was written: "The spirit of the Lord is upon me; therefore he has anointed me. He has sent me to bring glad tidings to the poor, to proclaim liberty to captives, recovery of sight to the blind and release of prisoners, to announce a year of favor from the Lord." Rolling up the scroll he gave it back to the assistant and sat down. All in the synagogue had their eyes fixed on him. Then he began by saying to them, "Today this Scripture passage is fulfilled in your hearing" (Luke 4:17–21).

In this passage Jesus proclaims the messianic era (he is the "anointed one") and, simultaneously, declares that that era is to begin as a jubilee year with the prescriptions that the poor (who have been disinherited from their land base) shall rejoice because of a new lease on life (and land), and that captives and prisoners are to be released.

(We may reflect once again here on Jesus' admonition about the sabbatical year, that his followers should not worry about what they would eat or drink, because God would provide: since the jubilee year was also a sabbatical year, when Jesus and his followers tried to live according to its prescriptions, times would be hard—especially if they were the only people living according to the jubilee commands! Thus, he comforted them with the promise of God's loving care. Because God cares for them God will send the Messiah to them, and because God cares for them God will satisfy their needs.)

For Jesus, the messianic era had direct social implications. The Messiah came to teach people obedience to God's commands, which included justice among peoples. The economic changes which Jesus proclaimed would bring about that justice, in part. Jesus takes up the jubilee theme again in the Lord's Prayer, the "Our Father," when he teaches his followers to pray:

> Give us this day our daily bread (Matthew 6:11)

and:

> Forgive us our debts,
> as we also have forgiven our debtors (Matthew 6:12; cf. Luke
> 11:4).

Jesus reaffirms God's providence in the jubilee year (the gift of food), the freeing of slaves (who became slaves because they had to sell themselves and their families to pay off debts) and the cancellation of all debts. In effect, those who pray the Lord's Prayer are asking God to forgive them their debts (offenses against God) to the extent that they forgive others their monetary debts, to the extent that they observe the jubilee year.

The underlying message reiterated in the jubilee year prescriptions is that the land which belongs to God has been entrusted by God to *all* the people, to meet their needs, and that if individual families lost their legacy of land because of poorer soil quality, natural disasters such as droughts, insect plagues or floods, mismanagement, or family tragedies such as the premature loss of a head of household, they would have the chance to start anew every fifty years. God's intention was to ensure land for *all* the people, through its periodic redistribution, and so prevent the emergence of a landed aristocracy whose members appropriated for themselves not only the land and its fruits but also, because of their consequent economic and political power, the very dominion of God.

GLEANING

God intended for the Jewish people to care for each other on the land. While the sabbatical year was to aid the land's productivity and promote respect for it, and the jubilee year was to aid in its distribution, the practice of *gleaning* was to provide the fruits of the land for the landless poor. It was a way in which the hungry could gather food for themselves, and simultaneously a reminder that the fruits of the land were not just to be harvested and sold to benefit landholders.

The poor's right to glean is affirmed several times in the Old Testament. In Leviticus 19:9–10 (cf. 23:22) we hear God command:

> When you reap the harvest of your land, you shall not be so thorough that you reap the field to its very edge, nor shall you glean the stray ears of grain. Likewise, you shall not pick your vineyard bare, nor gather up the grapes that have fallen. These things you shall leave for the poor and the alien. I, the Lord, am your God.

In Deuteronomy 24:19–22, slightly different imagery is used:

> When you reap the harvest in your field and overlook a sheaf there, you shall not go back to get it; let it be for the

alien, the orphan or the widow, that the Lord, your God, may bless you in all your undertakings. When you knock down the fruit of your olive trees, you shall not go over the branches a second time; let what remains be for the alien, the orphan and the widow. When you pick your grapes, you shall not go over the vineyard a second time; let what remains be for the alien, the orphan and the widow. For remember that you were once slaves in Egypt; that is why I command you to observe this rule.

In both passages, the right of the poor to food, to the fruits of the land, is affirmed. The different crops mentioned symbolize satisfaction of the basic needs of food and drink, of bread and cooking oil.

In the beautiful biblical story of Ruth, the right to glean and the right to redeem family land are described. Ruth (a Moabite) returns with Naomi, her mother-in-law (a Jewess) to Bethlehem, leaving behind her family and culture. The impoverished women need food there, so Ruth asks Naomi, "Let me go and glean ears of grain in the field of anyone who will allow me that favor" (Ruth 2:2). Naomi grants her request, and Ruth ends up picking in the fields of Boaz, who she does not realize is a relative of Naomi. Boaz is attracted to her, shares his meal with her, and tells his servants to let her glean even from among the harvested sheaves and to drop handfuls of grain for her to gather. Boaz decides to marry Ruth, but by Israelite law he must first allow another relative, closer in blood ties to Naomi, to marry Ruth. That relative also would have the right to redeem the family land Naomi had sold to pay her debts. The other kinsman declines to redeem the land and marry Ruth, so Boaz does so. They become the great-grandparents of David, and thus are ancestors of Jesus.

In the New Testament, the right of the poor to glean in order to satisfy their hunger not only is affirmed but also is given precedence over the strict laws prohibiting harvesting on the sabbath, the sabbatical year and the jubilee year. In Exodus 20:8–11, the Jews are commanded, "Remember to keep holy the sabbath day," and are forbidden by God to labor on the sabbath or to allow their families, their animals, or even the non-Jews among them to do so. In Leviticus 25, as we have seen, harvesting is forbidden during the sabbatical and jubilee years. Yet the Synoptic Gospels show the concern of Jesus, a Jew, for his hungry apostles, also Jews, to the extent that he justifies their breaking of the strict Jewish sabbath law:

> It happened that he was walking through standing grain on the sabbath, and his disciples began to pull off heads of grain as they went along. At this the Pharisees protested: "Look! Why do they do a thing not permitted on the sabbath?" He said to them: "Have you never read what David did when he was in need and he and his men were hungry? How he entered God's house in the days of Abiathar the high priest and ate the holy bread which only the priests were permitted to eat? He even gave it to his men." Then he said to them: "The sabbath was made for man, not man for the sabbath" (Mark 2:23–27; cf. Matthew 12:1–8 and Luke 6:1–5; for David's action, see 1 Samuel 21:2–7).

For Jesus, the needs of the hungry were to be met by those who had plenty. He could inspire hope:

> Blest are you who hunger;
> you shall be filled (Luke 6:20)

and fear:

> Woe to you who are full;
> you shall go hungry (Luke 6:25).

And he could condemn the person who hoarded food and selfishly appropriated the wealth of the land:

> There was a rich man who had a good harvest. "What shall I do?" he asked himself. "I have no place to store my harvest. I know!" he said. "I will pull down my grain bins and build

larger ones. All my grain and my goods will go there. Then I will say to myself, 'You have blessings in reserve for years to come. Relax! Eat heartily, drink well. Enjoy yourself.' " But God said to him, "You fool! This very night your life shall be required of you. To whom will all this piled up wealth of yours go?" That is the way it works with the man who grows rich for himself instead of growing rich in the sight of God (Luke 12:16–21).

Jesus also condemned the rich man who did not feed the poor man, Lazarus, who lay hungry and ill outside his door (Luke 16:19–31). He warned his followers, "You cannot give yourself to God and money" (Luke 16:13) and told them: "The poor you will always have with you" (Mark 14:7) to care for. In all of this, Jesus is rooted firmly in the Old Testament prophetic tradition. Just as he proclaimed that religious laws could become secondary to human need ("the sabbath is made for man"), God declared to the Israelites through the prophet Isaiah:

> What care I for the number of your sacrifices? says the Lord.... When you come in to visit me, who asks these things of you?... Your hands are full of blood! Wash yourselves clean! Put away your misdeeds from before my eyes; cease doing evil; learn to do good. Make justice your aim: redress the wronged, hear the orphan's plea, defend the widow (1:11, 12, 15–16).

And again:

> Is this the manner of fasting I wish, of keeping a day of penance: that a man bow his head like a reed, and lie in sackcloth and ashes? Do you call this a fast, a day acceptable to the Lord? This, rather, is the fasting that I wish: releasing those bound unjustly, untying the thongs of the yoke; setting free the oppressed, breaking every yoke; sharing your bread with the hungry, sheltering the oppressed and the homeless; clothing the naked when you see them, and not turning your back on your own. Then your light shall break forth like the dawn... (58:5–8).

The right of the poor to food, then, is a recurring theme in the Scriptures. Gleaning was a minimal means employed by landholders to acknowledge that right.

A PILGRIM PERSPECTIVE

We are pilgrims on a journey. We travel from birth to death in time and from place to place in space. As we journey in time and space, our lives touch other lives and are touched by them in turn. If we come to see ourselves as pilgrims, and others as our fellow travelers upon an earth we all claim as home, we realize that we have here neither an eternal nor an infinite abode. We are here for but a moment in time. We are sustained by a planet with limited resources that are dedicated to all of its life forms for all of its life span. We have inherited the earth in trust from God; our children will inherit it in turn. We are responsible for passing it on to them in such a state as will enable it to provide for their needs from its bounty. We are the land's stewards, those who care for it on behalf of God, its ultimate sovereign, for our own and future generations.

We who realize that we are pilgrims and stewards recognize that our claim on the earth and its resources is not absolute: neither as individuals nor as a generation do we have the right to appropriate for ourselves what God has given to all. We must learn and live the biblical teaching that we should relate to the land and to each other in a spirit of harmony and of sharing. Our harmony with the land and each other will be appropriate for us, we who are images of God, because God is in harmony with the earth, able to make even untilled or seemingly unproductive land provide for human and animal needs. Our sharing of the land and its fruits is required of us as children of God because God's ultimate dominion over the land and God's stewardship mandate to us demand of us a non-proprietary attitude toward the earth and its gifts. We who are pilgrims must be concerned about the well-being of other travelers over the earth, who are tied to us by a common human bond and a common transitory earthly existence. We who are stewards must care about the needs of our global and generational human family, of our brothers and sisters of this and future times. We who are pilgrims and stewards recognize these things; the future of the earth and its creatures depends on how we live them.

chapter four

An American Heritage

*   *   *

When we travel through some parts of rural America, we see no evidence of the problems faced by the vast majority of farmers. The fields are lush and verdant, the houses and barns freshly painted, the silos reaching impressively upward, the livestock grazing contentedly, the whole scene under the watchful eye of the farm dog. How could family farmers be disappearing? How could farmland be consolidating? And, even if such be the case, why should we object? Is this not the American way, to allow "free enterprise" to take its course, to reward the hard-working?

The answers to our questions contradict what seems to be reality or common knowledge. The prosperous farms we see are those of the remnant farmers, those who are barely surviving or are large scale operators; or the farms belong to an investment company and are merely managed by those dwelling in the farmhouse. In 1935, there were 6.8 million U.S. farms, but by 1974 there were only 2.34 million. The average farm size went from 197 acres in 1940 to 440 acres in 1974.

Consolidation means fewer and fewer people control more and more land: 25% of all private landholders own 97% of all private land. Of the 2.3 billion acres of land in the U.S. (excluding Alaska), more than half are farmland. Just 3% of the total U.S. population own all of the farmland, and just 0.14% of the total U.S. population (5 percent of farmland owners) owns 48.1% of all farmland. Thus, that same *0.14% of the total U.S.*

population owns about 24% of all of the land in the United States! Such startling figures, unknown to most Americans and with unpleasant implications for *all* Americans, contradict the American dream and the American heritage. They led the United States Department of Agriculture (USDA) to conclude in its report, *A Time To Choose* (1981):

> If present trends continue, landownership will become more concentrated, with increased separation between the ownership and use of the land—that is, an increase in absentee ownership and a corollary increase in tenant farmland.

The United States seems headed, in other words, to a situation in which a landed aristocracy will own—and therefore control—the nation's land base. Should such a state come to pass, it would be ironic indeed. Our country was founded for the most part by people seeking an alternative to a European economic system in which a hereditary minority owned and controlled land on which worked the disinherited majority. The founders of the United States, and many legislators over the past two centuries, tried to create an alternative to the large hereditary estates of Europe. They tried to provide, as much as possible, for widespread distribution of land ownership and the opportunity for every citizen to own some part of the country. As we shall see, a consistent idea underlying much government land legislation from colonial times through the present has been this: that the land is an *American* heritage, not the property of a few, and that every citizen should be able to have a definite stake in that heritage.

In the early history of the United States there was no understanding of the limited nature of the heritage of land. The population was sparse for the vast North American continent. It was assumed that more land could be obtained through purchase or conquest, and people could just move west and appropriate for themselves new property. Once the national boundaries were firmly established, however, and the population began to multiply, a new realization entered into the American consciousness: *the land was limited,* and its ownership and use somehow must be regulated if the old European reality was not to become the new American reality. From a lack of concern about unlimited land, policy-makers became concerned about diminishing land. They realized that if the basic principle of land as an American heritage were to be preserved, then government intervention—the intervention of the people as a whole for the people as individuals—would be necessary.

THE NEW NATION

After the hectic and trying days of the American Revolution, the leaders and artisans of the new republic were confronted by a task that was perhaps even more difficult than had been the Revolutionary War: to lay the foundation of a completely new social order. In the laws and writings of the early days of the United States, the first struggles of that task might be seen.

One of the major issues the new government had to deal with was land ownership. Conscious of the inequalities existing in Europe, the first government officials sought to provide a stake in the land for as extensive a number of citizens as possible. Thus, shortly after the promulgation of the Northwest Ordinance in 1787, Congress set up land offices in surveyed regions of the new territory in order to promote sales of land to individual proprietors. The law provided for the establishment of townships that were to be six miles square. Each township was to have thirty-six sections of one square mile each. (Over time a quarter section, one hundred and sixty acres, was accepted as homestead size, and Congress passed a law to that effect in 1804.) Concern for the new citizen as a potential landholder, having a right to a part of the new country, was seen also in the early tax structure that was established. *The first direct tax levied by the United States government was a graduat-*

ed tax imposed on urban land. The tax law, passed in 1798, decreed that as acreage increased, so did the tax rate. The graduated land tax later disappeared, but one of its provisions might still be seen today: the "homestead exemption" that allows a family base of land to be untaxed. What made the tax even more remarkable (and what helped lead eventually to its repeal) was the fact that many of the early framers of U.S. legislation were significant landholders themselves. For a while, at least, they rose above narrow self-interest to promote the broader public interest, the right of all citizens to share the soil and its fruits. What still lived, in those early legislative years, was the spirit of democracy of property ownership that had been proclaimed by such revolutionary stalwarts as Thomas Paine and Thomas Jefferson.

THOMAS PAINE

In two of his major treatises, Thomas Paine discussed the question of land as property: "The Rights of Man, Part Second" (1792); and "Agrarian Justice" (1796).

In "The Rights of Man," Paine declares that "there ought to be a limit to property, or the accumulation of it by bequest." He calls the wealth of vast estates "a prohibitable luxury" when it goes far beyond what is "necessary or sufficient for the support of a family." Therefore, he says, wealth from estates should be progressively taxed. He believed that this tax would help to break up and reapportion vast estates, and operate to "extirpate the unjust and unnatural law of primogeniture, and the vicious influence of the aristocratical system." His hope was that the poor would come into their rightful inheritance, because only when the poor are out of distress may a nation "boast of its constitution and its government."

Paine expanded on his ideas somewhat in "Agrarian Justice," in which he states that "the earth, in its natural, uncultivated state, was, and ever would have continued to be, *the common property of the human race.* In that state every man would have been born to property" [emphasis in original]. Paine notes that since the uncultivated earth could not support as many inhabitants as cultivated land, the "civilized state" is necessary. Since it is impossible to separate the improvements on the land from the land itself, landed property arose; but in reality, "it is the value of the improvement, only, and not the earth itself, that is individual property." He declares that since people have not created the earth, they have no right to have any part of it as their property in perpetuity, for "neither did the Creator of the earth open a land office, from whence the first title-deeds should issue." Paine states that the present possessors of the land cannot be faulted, for they did not create the system which brought them vast holdings. However, the land must be redistributed, and he proposes an inheritance tax as the means to do so.

Paine believed that to change property relations the intervention of government is necessary because of the *reluctance of the rich*—"With respect to justice, it ought not to be left to the choice of detached individuals whether they will do justice or not"—and the *plight of the poor*—"The great mass of the poor in all countries are becoming an hereditary race, and it is next to impossible for them to get out of that state of themselves." Paine observes that "the accumulation of personal property is, in many instances, the effect of paying too little for the labor that produced it."

For Thomas Paine, then, there existed an inequitable distribution of land. It was necessary to limit property, and its accumulation by bequest, through an inheritance tax and a graduated land tax. By these measures, the poor could acquire a share in the land which belonged to them and all people as "the common property of the human race." For Paine, the federal government had the responsibility to redress property inequalities, some of which had resulted because people were unjustly recompensed for their labors. In Paine's writings we can see the seeds of existing present-day inheritance taxes and minimum wage laws, and the proposed graduated land tax advocated by some farmer and church organizations.

THOMAS JEFFERSON

The principal architect (and principles' architect) of the new social structure that began to come into being through the Declaration of Independence of July 4, 1776 was Thomas Jefferson, a Virginia landholder. In that Declaration, for which he was primarily responsible, Jefferson proclaimed with the other founders of American democracy the theoretical base of the new nation; the "self-evident" truths that "all men are created equal, that they are endowed by their Creator with certain unalienable Rights, that among these are Life, Liberty, and the pursuit of Happiness—that to secure these rights, Governments are instituted. . . ."

When he reflected on the land question, Jefferson sought to guarantee the "unalienable rights" through the power of government. He had seen the economic and political inequalities extant in Europe, inequalities largely attributable to an economic system and land distribution that maintained the wealth and power of a landed aristocracy. He did not want a similar state to come to pass in the new country.

Jefferson wrote that "the earth is given as a common stock for man to labor and live on." This common stock should best be distributed as widely as possible, because "the small land holders are the most precious part of the state." Jefferson thought that agriculture was the best way of life, and hoped that Americans would engage in farming as long as possible because cultivators of the soil were the best citizens. He kept a "Garden Book" from age twenty-three on, and a "Farm Book" from age thirty-one on. He disapproved of absentee ownership and crops that wasted the land (among which he counted tobacco), and advocated crop rotation in an age when large landholders would deplete one area's soil and then move on to a new plot of land. He had a policy on his own lands of not planting corn more than once every five years on the same site, because of the way it affected the soil. He declared that "those who labour in the earth are the chosen people of God. . . ." By the time he died, Jefferson belonged to almost every agricultural society in the United States and some in Europe. He always supported farmers (including those involved in Shay's Rebellion, part of which was directed at preventing foreclosures and sheriffs' sales of land). In his travels abroad, he constantly looked for new crop possibilities (such as olive trees and rice) for the developing United States agriculture.

Jefferson's love for the land and for farming as a way of life, coupled with his democratic ideals, led him to propose ways by which more people might become landholders. In a letter to the Rev. James Madison (in 1795) he suggested that a way to lessen the "inequality of property" would be "to exempt all from taxation below a certain point and to tax the higher portions of property in geometrical progression as they rise. . . ." The right of all to land would be fostered by protecting ownership of family-sized property and encouraging the sale of larger holdings for new family-sized holdings, all through a progressive property tax having a homestead exemption. For Jefferson, then, the number and security of the small landholders, "the most precious part of the state," were to be promoted. John Adams, another founder of the American republic, voiced a similar sentiment when he stated that "if the lands are held and owned by the people, and prevented from drifting into one or a few hands, the true power will rest with the people, and that government will, essentially, be a democracy. . . ." One might see in the thrust of these statements a firm belief in the need for people to have some recognized roots in the soil, some minimum land base to provide them security and from which they might have the freedom to forge their own future. Without that base, without that freedom, they would be at the mercy of those that did own or control the land. Thus they would lose their political freedom and with that loss democracy would disappear and the dream of the American Revolution be dissipated and destroyed.

THE TRADITION STRENGTHENED

The sentiments of the founders of the American republic were echoed in the legislation enacted in ensuing years. A series of laws were passed to promote family-sized holdings and, presumably, to foster to some extent both political and economic democracy.

The *Pre-Emption Acts* of 1830, 1832, 1834, 1838, and 1840 forgave squatters for settling on public lands illegally, and allowed them to purchase the occupied lands, without competitive bidding, at the minimum price—$1.25 per acre—established by the government, and the 1841 Pre-Emption Act opened all surveyed public lands to squatting. Thus, squatters who cultivated the land and built houses on it were allowed to own it. Previously, troops had been used to expel them and burn their houses or shacks. The *Swamp Land Act* (1850) provided that public lands in forty acre tracts that were flooded at either planting or harvest time were to be granted to the states, which in turn were to use the money obtained from their sale to reclaim them, The *Morrill Act* (1862) set aside funds in the public trust, in every state of the nation, to be used for agricultural and mechanical colleges.

The *Homestead Act* (1862) passed by a Republican administration in the midst of the Civil War, represented a major government effort to promote widespread ownership of lands newly opened to settlement. The Act provided that any citizen, or any person who said that he or she would become a citizen (if twenty-one years old, or a head of family if not twenty-one), could acquire a 160-acre tract of land by residing on that land for five years and making some improvements upon it; no payment was necessary for the land. A separate provision allowed a settler to gain title after only six months' residence if improvements were made and $1.25 per acre were paid. The Homestead Act helped to foster the family farm system of agriculture that took firm root in the midwest, a system in sharp contrast to such other agricultural systems as the southern plantation system and the large family estates of Latin America and the American southwest. The act originally had been vetoed by Democratic President James Buchanan in 1850 as being "communistic."

The *Timber Culture Act* (1873) granted tracts of one hundred and sixty acres of land to those who would plant at least forty acres of trees on each tract. (In 1878, the number was reduced to ten acres of trees.) The *Desert Land Act* (1877) promoted irrigation of arid lands on tracts of up to six hundred and forty acres (later reduced to three hundred and twenty acres). The *Hatch Act* (1887) appropriated money to establish agricultural experiment stations to aid farmers in increasing the quality and quantity of their production. The *Carey Act* (1894) granted federal public lands to the states to be used to develop irrigation systems and to be sold to homesteaders.

Laws intended to support family-sized holdings continued into the twentieth century. The *Reclamation Act* (1902) provided that money obtained from the sale of public lands would be used to finance irrigation in dry areas. In fulfillment of the Act, such projects as Roosevelt Dam in Arizona, Elephant Butte Dam in New Mexico, and Arrowrock Dam in Idaho were constructed. The Act specified that lands irrigated by federally funded water projects were to be limited to one hundred and sixty-acre homesteads. The intent, again, was to promote widespread ownership of the national heritage. The *Smith-Lever Act* (1914) established the cooperative extension service to educate people in agricultural practices and home economics, thereby to promote better farm conditions. The *Federal Farm Loan Act* (1916) granted low-interest credit to farmers. The *Capper-Volstead Act* (1922) encouraged the organization of farmers' groups by exempting agricultural cooperatives from compliance with antitrust laws. The *Agricultural Marketing Act* (1929) set up a major farm support program that included loans to farm organizations to construct storage facilities to hold food surpluses until farmers could get a better price for their produce. The *Agricultural Adjustment Acts* (1933 and 1938) and the *Soil Conservation and Domestic Allotment Act* (1936) attempted to restrict crop production, in order to help farmers obtain higher prices for their produce by paying farmers for not planting crops on part of their holdings. The *Bankhead-Jones Farm Tenancy Act* (1937) was enacted to aid tenant (rentor) farmers and low-income farmers to become secure land owners and to purchase agricultural equipment. The Act set up a Farm Security Administration in the United States Department of Agriculture to provide loans and insured mortgages. Later, the Farmers' Home Administration was established (1946) to replace the Farm Security Administration. There were also some slight efforts made to aid migrant workers within the United States. The Truman Report (by the Commission on Migratory Labor appointed by President Truman in 1950) recommended that farmworkers be covered by minimum wage laws, have decent housing provided for them and be protected from child labor exploitation. The report was followed by *Public Law 78* (1952) which restricted employment of alien laborers to those numbers certified by the Secretary of Labor as necessary in particular areas where the local labor force was insufficient, provided also that local workers' wages and working conditions would not be negatively influenced by the influx of alien workers.

THE SPIRIT OF THE LAW

The intent of all of the legislation cited, from the Revolutionary Era to the present day, was to foster widespread ownership of the American land heritage. The spirit of the law, as well as the letter of the law, was to establish a stake in the land base for a broad constituency. Those who had no working relationship with the land, even those who lived in urban centers, were to be given the opportunity to acquire land. Those who owned land were to be made secure in their ownership. And those who worked the land as rentors or migratory laborers were to have access to owning and working for themselves the land they worked for others. The spirit and the trend were plain to see: distribute the land as much as possible; help the land's broad-based constituents to have stability of ownership.

In the years from the American Revolution through the Great Depression of the 1930's, the spirit of the law was proclaimed—at times quite forcefully—by citizens who wished to secure what they perceived to be their birthright.

One of the first problems the new government faced shortly after the Revolution was a series of rebellions or acts of

civil disobedience by farmers—most of them veterans of the
Revolutionary War—who felt that they were being unjustly
treated by the new government. In some cases, veterans who
had not been paid for their service to their country were put
into debtor's prison on their return to their homes because
they lacked the money to pay their debts. The government,
which did not pay them their due on the one hand, exacted
money from them on the other. The outraged veterans began
organizing farmers into military units to prevent wealthy landholders and bankers from using the court system to seize farmers' lands and throw farmers into debtor's prison. Sometimes
(in scenes which would later be repeated in the Great Depression) the armed farmers kept the local courts from meeting.
Among the disgruntled farmers was Daniel Shays, from western Massachusetts, a wounded veteran of the battles of Lexing-
ton, Bunker Hill, and Saratoga. Shays and his ragged farmers
fought several times with the militia in what came to be
known as Shays' rebellion (1780–81). Finally defeated, he was
condemned to death but later pardoned. The founders of the
United States, with the exception of Thomas Jefferson, were
appalled by the rebellions even though they themselves had
broken the law to become free of the king of England's control. One of Washington's veterans, General Henry Knox, complained that the rebels believed that "the property of the
United States has been protected from the confiscations of
Britain by the joint exertions of all, and therefore ought to be
the common property of all." Jefferson, in support of Shays,
wrote from France (where he was then serving as U.S. ambas-
sador) that "a little rebellion now and then is a good thing,"
and that "the tree of liberty must be refreshed from time to
time with the blood of patriots and tyrants." In one of history's
ironies, the "patriots" in this case were rebellious farmers and
the "tyrants" were members (most of them wealthy landholders) of the new government that was proclaiming liberty and
justice!

The spirit of the law, the spirit that declared the land to be
a common inheritance, was expressed again in succeeding
years. The *Mechanics Free Press* newspaper urged in 1821 that

public land be held for eventual donation to U.S. citizens. In 1822, the great orator Daniel Webster declared, after New England states had abolished laws of primogeniture and entails, that "the consequence of all these causes has been a great subdivision of the soil and a great equality of condition, the true basis, most certainly, of a popular government." In 1823, President James Monroe stated what came to be known as the Monroe Doctrine when he declared the Americas off-limits to European colonial domination—in effect affirming on an international level a wider distribution of property in land. A pamphlet by Thomas Skidmore in 1829, *Rights of Man to Property,* stated that the unequal distribution of property in land was the basis of social injustice, the remedy for which was to abolish land inheritances.

In 1848, a handbill distributed by labor organizations declared: "Are you an American citizen? Then you are a joint owner of the public lands. Why not take enough of your property to provide yourself a home? Why not vote yourself a farm?" The pamphlet condemned the "aristocracy of avarice" and urged formation of an "American party" whose "chief measures will be first to limit the quantity of land that any one man henceforth monopolize or inherit; and second to make public lands free to actual settlers only. . . ." The slogan "Vote yourself a farm!" was widely used by labor groups and political aspirants in the mid-to-late nineteenth century. A similar sentiment prompted newspaper publisher Horace Greeley's famous 1851 statement, "Go west, young man, go west!" Greeley was encouraging urban factory workers to acquire homesteads. In the pages of his New York *Tribune,* he also advocated breaking up New York manors and taxing single ownership of lands in excess of three hundred and twenty acres, in order to promote their sale and wider distribution.

In 1854, Gerrit Smith, a U.S. Representative from New York who had campaigned in 1852 in part on a platform that declared "The right to the soil is as natural and equal as the right to light and air," introduced some land-related resolutions in the House of Representatives during discussion of the proposed Homestead Act. In his resolutions he stated that the

Congress had no right to dispose of public lands (the people's legacy) by sale or gift. Government's duty was only to regulate occupation of the lands, and "this regulation should ever proceed on the principle that the right of all persons to the soil—to the great source of human subsistence—is as equal, as inherent, and as sacred, as the right to life itself. . . ." Smith said that a person might dispose, as producer, of the fruits of the soil, but "no such right can he have in the soil itself." He feared that a few persons might eventually come to monopolize a town, a county, the nation, and even the entire earth, and use their land "for the enjoyment of the aristocracy." Smith thus expressed the recurring public fear that land consolidation meant loss of economic power and thus, ultimately, of political power as well. (For a fuller description of the American tradition of land distribution, see Aaron M. Sakolski's *Land Tenure and Land Taxation in America*.)

HENRY GEORGE AND THE "SINGLE TAX"

Shortly after the Civil War, the journalist-economist-philosopher Henry George began to speak out against the monopolization of the land's wealth. In 1871 he published a book entitled *Our Land and Land Policy*. George believed that a tax should be imposed only on the unearned increment of increased land value. In his 1879 book *Progress and Poverty* he developed his ideas more thoroughly, in such a way that would eventually influence the later land taxation systems of such nations as Israel and Australia. George opposed rent of land, nationalization of land, and communism. He believed that land, the basis of wealth, was becoming monopolized. His solution to poverty and land consolidation was a "single tax," a tax on land (on the value it gained incrementally through speculation or inflation, regardless of improvements). He thought that this "single tax" would aid wider distribution of the land by creating economic pressure for people to put unused land on the market. (George also advocated "equal pay for equal work for women," and ran for mayor of New York City in 1886 in the

Independent Labor Party, coming in second to Democrat Abram Hewitt but ahead of the Republican nominee, Theodore Roosevelt, who came in third.) George believed that the "single tax" would replace all other taxes on labor and goods and still be able to raise sufficient funds to meet government needs and eliminate poverty.

For Henry George, "Historically, as ethically, private property in land is robbery." There can be "no just title to an exclusive possession of the soil. . . . Private property in land is a bold, bare, enormous wrong, like that of chattel slavery." George made a distinction between ultimate ownership of the land and ultimate ownership of improvements on it: "Let the landholders retain their improvements and personal property in secure possession." Thus, the land itself belonged equally to all people, but improvements upon it belonged to those who made them. George did not propose land expropriation: ". . . it is not necessary in order to secure equal rights to land to make an equal division of land. All that it is necessary to do is to collect rent for the common benefit." Since "the unequal ownership of land necessitates the unequal distribution of wealth," land as common property would promote the equal distribution of wealth. Again, George did not propose expropriation of either the land or its improvements. In his view, common ownership of the former (as represented by the land tax, a rent to the community whose benefits would be equitably distributed throughout the community) and economic incentives for the latter (the desire for profit and well-being, which did not require ownership of the land but only of its improvements and products) would be most consonant with a recognition that land was the common inheritance of all people. George proposed that if land were taxed according to its inherent value, then landholders would be encouraged to improve the land (from which improvements they might make their profit) or to sell it to others who would improve it. Thus, improvements would not be fined (as in the present property tax structure), but encouraged. Farmers would be greatly aided in that their machinery and buildings would not be taxed, while the amount of tax on the value of their base land would be less than that of the same amount of urban land, since city land values were higher than rural land values. Henry George's proposals, then, were an attempt to establish a specific means to promote the American tradition that the land was for the benefit of society as a whole, not for the profit of a few individuals.

AGRICULTURAL MOVEMENTS

Americans' right to land has been most consistently advocated by those who have had the most immediate relationship to the soil, those who—figuratively as well as literally—planted roots deep in it: the farmers. Although they prided themselves in having an "independence" they felt was not shared by their city cousins, many farmers did, nonetheless, band into organizations to secure their way of life against the vagaries of nature and the avarice of the greedy.

One of the earliest organized movements of farmers was the Grange, or Patrons of Husbandry, founded in 1867 chiefly to curb the power of railroad companies and grain elevators. The latter companies charged excessive rates or cheated farmers of a profitable return on their produce. Some of the company practices such as excessive rail shipping rates and elevator operators mixing grades (paying the farmer a low price for a lower grade of grain such as wheat, then mixing part of that with a higher grade in quantities that made the total qualify as a higher grade and therefore able to be resold at a higher price) deprived farmers of a fair return on their labors. The grangers were able to pressure state governments for remedial legislation that more closely regulated the shipping process, and to ensure adherence to that legislation through court action. The grangers also set up the first farmers' cooperatives which, although forced out of business, did pave the way for future such efforts to bypass the middlemen and secure a higher price for farm goods.

During the Depression of 1877, another farmers' movement began: the Farmers Alliance. Originating in Texas, the Alliance philosophy expanded nationwide until three thousand

Alliances existed in 1887. The Alliance farmers took up anew the cooperative movement. They used cooperatives both to buy seed and equipment at lower prices and to sell their produce at higher prices. The Farmers Alliance also developed ties with the labor movement and such of its organizations as the Knights of Labor. By 1890, the various Alliances had become active in political campaigns, and in that year had full or at least partial control of the legislatures of twelve states. (The Populist Party would spring up in a few years from the Farmers Alliance.) Among the planks of Alliance political platforms was the advocacy of federal produce warehouses where farmers could store their produce at little or no cost, receive loan certificates based on the value of that produce, sell the produce when prices went up and then pay back the loan to the government at low interest. The struggle to effect political change also brought together as allies black and white farmers, the former having their own Colored Farmers Alliance. Efforts were made to create a new culture through the formation of the Alliance Lecture Bureau. Through all of these means, Alliance farmers protested against the ideology and practices of those whom they saw to be bringing them to ruin, forcing them off their American heritage of land.

In the twentieth century, new agricultural organizations continued to be founded to meet the expanding needs of farmers, tenants, and farmworkers.

In 1902, the Farmer's Educational and Cooperative Union of America was founded, later to become known as the Farmers Union. The Farmers Union stressed cooperatives: cooperative buying of farm inputs and cooperative selling of farm products. The Farmers Union is one of the largest farm organizations today, having more actual farmer members than most other farm organizations. Besides its work with cooperatives, the Farmers Union works to effect state and national legislation beneficial to family farmers.

The most well known of the farm organizations, because of its economic power and consequent political clout, is the American Farm Bureau Federation or Farm Bureau. The Farm Bureau had its origins in 1911 in the Broome County

Chamber of Commerce, headquartered in Binghamton, New York. The Chamber formed an agricultural committee which was separated in 1914 as the Broome County Farm Bureau. Then, as now, the Farm Bureau has been the advocate of the interests of large, wealthy farmers, who comprise the dominant force among farmer members of the organization. Its insurance programs have attracted into membership operators of small- and moderate-sized farms, as well as many non-farmers. (The claims of farmer representation by the Farm Bureau must be questioned when its figures of farmer membership exceed the total number of actual farmers counted by government surveys—and most farmers probably do not hold membership in the Farm Bureau.) The Farm Bureau opposes most government intervention into agriculture (except such intervention as the federal tax laws and federally funded research projects that are geared toward large operators), believing basically in a "survival of the fittest" or "free enterprise" agricultural economy.

Other agricultural organizations, in contrast, have been oriented toward and speak on behalf of family farmers. The Southern Tenant Farmers Union was founded in 1934 to protect the rights of southern rentors and sharecroppers. It was unique for its day in that it was a close alliance of both black and white farmers (which caused its members to suffer harassment, beatings, and murder). The STFU later became the National Farm Labor Union and then a member of the American Federation of Labor, continuing its work but in association with urban unions.

In 1952, the United States Farmers Association was formed. The USFA has as its slogan "Peace, Parity and Power to the People!" and, more than any other farm organization, relates U.S. agricultural issues to broader national and international issues. It advocates some government support for farmers, but focuses on better prices for farm goods through parity (the ratio between farm costs and income, usually geared to its years of top benefit to the farmer, 1910–1914, when a higher profit was made) and support for consumers through a national Consumers' Protection Agency. In a 1980 *U.S. Farm News* newspaper, the USFA outlined its underlying philosophy after listing problems of civil rights and militarism:

> The leaders of the Association don't believe that the farm problem can be detached from these other problems. . . . It is inter-related with other economic, social and political problems and the domestic problems are related to international problems.
>
> The struggle to maintain security and freedom on the land for the farm families in America is today a part of a world struggle that can be resolved only through general and complete world disarmament so that the billions spent for arms and bombs can be channeled into peaceful uses to raise the standard of living for all the people in an economy of balanced abundance.

The USFA continues today as the most progressive and globally conscious farm organization.

In 1955, the National Farmers Organization originated in Iowa. Its major thrust distinguished it from other farm groups: a focus on collective bargaining for farmers. The NFO believes that farmers should unite in the same way labor unions do and collectively bargain for the price they are to receive for their goods. The NFO consequently set up its own selling system, in competition with existing Boards of Trade and Exchanges, and gathers together at collection points its individual members' agricultural products, for sale in larger quantities to buyers. The NFO's larger total volume thus enables individual farmers to receive higher prices for their goods than they would obtain by themselves. The NFO believes in very limited government intervention, thinking that farmers who are organized well and market their goods together will be able to meet their own needs.

Other farmer organizations include the American Agriculture Movement (AAM), a loosely organized group of farmers founded in 1977 who advocate parity, put together the tractorcades to Washington, D.C. to protest government policies, and tried vainly to organize a farm strike; the Emergency Land

Fund (ELF), located in the south, an organization of black farmers trying to hold onto their land in the face of racial and economic pressures; National Land for People, in California, which tries to promote enforcement of legislation passed to aid family farms, such as the 1902 Reclamation Act; and the Center for Rural Affairs, in Walthill, Nebraska, which focuses on promoting family farms through educational programs on legislation, tax laws, and energy-saving agricultural practices.

Farmworkers, too, have fought for their rights on the land. Underpaid, suffering from malnutrition and ill health while picking the very food that would help them, picking in the hot sun for long hours of "stoop labor" with no toilet facilities and being sometimes sprayed with poisonous herbicides and pesticides, the farmworkers united in such unions as the United Farm Workers (UFW), under the leadership of Cesar Chavez, focusing primarily in California, Florida, and Texas; the Texas Farm Workers (TFW), a breakaway group from the UFW, headed by Antonio Orendain; and the Farm Labor Organizing Committee (FLOC), led by Baldemar Velasquez and working mainly in the midwestern United States.

In their efforts to secure justice on the land, farmers and farmworkers, confronted by government's partial measures and by agribusiness and other corporate pressures, organized themselves into interest groups. As a result of their efforts, they have been able to hold on to at least part of the American heritage of land and of land-conserving ideas and practices. They have had disagreements among themselves, but they have also been able to keep before legislators and the urban public an awareness of the pressures upon and needs of American farmers and farmworkers.

THE AMERICAN HERITAGE

A tradition that has been passed down through the history of the American republic states that the land is limited and is for everyone. It is the American heritage, the birthright of all who live and labor on it—all of us. It is our heritage in that it has been passed on to us by those who went before us. It is our heritage, too, in that a thrust of thought about the land, from the foundation of the republic to the present day, has been— on the levels both of ideas and of legislation—that the land belongs in a general way to all of us. Individual proprietorship has not generally been questioned, except when it came to be regarded as excessive. The land within our national borders, to the extent that it can be passed on from generation to generation (that is, to the extent that justice for American Indians and the ultimate ownership and dominion of God are recognized), is part of our common heritage.

We have seen, in contrast, how land ownership is becoming consolidated into fewer and fewer, but larger and larger, individual holdings. This present trend contradicts the principle of American lands as a national heritage. The nation's founders, in their foresight, saw what would happen if land ownership were to become concentrated in a few hands, under a few names, and tried to prevent that from happening. Being familiar with European feudalism, and the political power that accompanied the economic wealth tied to land ownership, they proposed limiting and redistributing large land holdings through government intervention. They realized that the wealthy wanted no change and that the poor were powerless to effect change, and so government must mediate the claims of the disinherited against a class of landed heirs. They proposed such means as a graduated land tax and an inheritance tax (with a homestead—family-size—exemption) to ensure widespread land ownership. National leaders, as well as rural (and even urban) grassroots movements in succeeding generations, continued the advocacy of widespread ownership and careful use of the land. They realized that widespread land distribution means greater democracy because a land base makes individuals more secure and freer to voice their individual or collective will.

Despite the witness of history, despite the tradition, land consolidation occurred. It resulted primarily from subversion of the spirit, if not the actual letter, of land legislation. In some cases the American people were defrauded of part of their inheritance before laws safeguarding it could be passed. In other cases, the ink was barely dry on new legislation before individuals and companies, and the lawyers that aided them both, found ways to circumvent it. In yet other cases, greedy speculators were supported by greedy politicians, and land-related laws were substantially amended or even erased entirely from the books. In all of these cases, the power of wealth overrode the well-being of the people. And because money generates money and poverty begets powerlessness, the truism that "the rich get richer and the poor get poorer" has held true in land ownership and use.

The land in America is part of the American people's heritage, just as the earth is part of the global human family's heritage. The heritage might be passed on as a physical inheritance: land itself is entrusted to those who work it to produce food and fiber for all of us. The heritage might also be passed on as a recognition of our common roots in and stake in the land: the land's benefits are distributed among those who do not directly work it.

A careful balance must be struck, if we are to be true to our American heritage, between common ultimate ownership of the land and individual civil ownership of the land. If such a balance is not maintained, either those who work the land or those who otherwise benefit from its fruits will be victims of injustice. That land ultimately belongs to the whole community does not mean that the community might exploit the producers of food, those who have immediate stewardship of the land. The exploitive relationship would put the community in the position of the old plantation owner, and the food producers in the position of slaves. In stark contrast to this is the understanding of the complementary of vocations, and so the complementarity of relationships with the land in a civil sense: the doctor, lawyer, teacher, mechanic, secretary, janitor, construction worker, and farmer complement each other in building up society, the total human community, and each should be justly compensated for the individual work rendered on behalf of that community. Thus, the cheap food policy that exploits farmers and farmworkers is as much an affront to the

American heritage as "free enterprise" policies that promote land consolidation. Both contradict the concept of community ownership of the land. Farmers are also a part of the community, with the same right to a moderate livelihood that physicians have. (Of course, in our present U.S. context, physicians receive, on the average, exorbitant, not moderate, compensation for their work, while farmers and farmworkers, in contrast, receive poor, not moderate, compensation.) And community members are also shareholders in the trust of land that is part of the American heritage, and so have a right to its fruits. Again, government must exercise its proper role as mediator between the competing and conflicting claims people make on their common American heritage. People, too, as individuals must remember that the government is supposed to be us, "we the people of the United States," just as public lands are supposed to be ours. If we wish to preserve our American heritage, we must, as citizens, use the power of our government to prevent its usurpation by a few: whether in terms of individual property holdings such as farm acreages or of collective property holdings such as forest acreages, the public lands of our national parks and forests.

The American heritage includes America's land and the tradition that says that the land is meant to benefit us all. In very direct ways, then, we can see similarities among the American heritage and the Native American and Judaeo-Christian heritages which both precede it and form part of it. Within the United States, different churches have reflected on and addressed themselves to the relationship among those heritages and traditions. In their statements, the heritages of a particular place—the United States—in a particular time—the twentieth century—converge and at times conflate.

chapter five

The Church and the Land

*   *   *

On October 4, 1979, in the heart of heartland America, Pope John Paul II addressed the multitudes gathered at the Living History Farms near Des Moines, Iowa for an outdoor Mass. In his homily he stressed the need for responsible stewardship of the land, particularly on the part of the heartland's farmers who were charged with the responsibility of caring for an especially productive part of the earth. To the hundreds of thousands of pilgrims who braved the windy cold, the Pope's message was clear: conserve the land well so that future generations would inherit an ever-richer earth.

Pope John Paul's Des Moines homily had several implications. In his personal history, it was one of a series of addresses or comments that he issued on land issues. Within the global Catholic Church, it represented another step in a long-standing tradition of concern for agrarian justice and reform. And, within its heartland context, it was another Catholic Church statement about the land, the latest of a series of documents expressing concern over land consolidation and abuse.

In its American context, the homily given by Pope John Paul was in the mainstream of recent Church documents on social justice in general and agrarian justice in particular. It was subsequent to the Appalachian bishops' land statement, *This Land is Home to Me;* and it preceded (although it was directly linked to) the midwestern bishops' statement, *Strangers and Guests—Toward Community in the Heartland.* In these and other documents, as well as in Pope John Paul's homily, the concept and responsibility of land stewardship are advocated.

HISTORIC CONCERN FOR THE LAND

The history of the Catholic church is a history of concern for the poor, the oppressed who are the ones with whom Jesus himself, as the Son of Man, wished to be identified: "For I was hungry, and you gave me to eat; thirsty, and you gave me drink; naked, and you clothed me; shelterless, and you took me in; sick or imprisoned, and you visited me.... As long as you did it to the least of my brethren, you did it to me" (Matthew 25:31–46). We have seen earlier how this tradition of concern for the downtrodden was manifest elsewhere in the Bible and the Christian Church. Among the Christians of the first few centuries, this concern was expressed in word and work, including in the way land was viewed. In the words of an early Christian writer, "The soil was given to the rich and the poor in common. The pagans hold land as property, and therefore blaspheme God." A thousand years later (and still almost a thousand years ago!), St. Thomas Aquinas would declare that "whatever people have in superabundance is due, by natural law, to the purpose of succoring the poor," and that in times of extreme necessity, "all things are common property," according to the natural law, and hence the poor oppressed might satisfy their hunger by taking from another's abundance.

RECENT PAPAL TEACHINGS

The voice of justice, speaking from the Church, continued through the centuries. In the late nineteenth century it would take the form of a major encyclical on social justice, *Rerum Novarum (On the Condition of Labor),* issued by Pope Leo XIII in 1891. Pope Leo spoke of the division of society into two "castes": one "which holds the power because it holds the wealth" and another comprised of "the needy and powerless multitude, sore and suffering." In addressing the problem of land ownership Pope Leo would query, "Is it just that the fruit of man's sweat and labor should be enjoyed by another?"— thus questioning property relations in which people could use, but not own, the land. In 1937 Pope Pius XI, in his encyclical *Divini Redemptoris (Atheistic Communism)*, would state that the rich were to consider themselves "only as stewards of their earthly goods." In a radio broadcast in 1941 commemorating the fiftieth anniversary of *Rerum Novarum*, Pope Pius XII would affirm an individual's "right to make use of the material goods of the earth," a right which is "from nature."

As papal perceptions of increasing world poverty, decreasing world resources and the concentration of the land and its resources into fewer and fewer hands have been heightened, papal pronouncements on those issues have been multiplied. John XXIII, Paul VI and, presently, John Paul II have all made land issues one of their social justice concerns.

Pope John XXIII stated in his encyclical *Mater et Magistra (Christianity and Social Progress)*, issued in 1961, that "the farming community is a depressed area," and it "must take an active part in its own economic advancement, social progress and cultural betterment." He declared that "rural workers should feel a sense of solidarity with one another, and should unite to form cooperatives and professional associations." He believed that we must "consider as an ideal the kind of farm which is owned and managed by the family" and undertake efforts to promote such farms. He deplored low wages for farmworkers, which kept them "in a permanent state of economic and social inferiority, depriving them of the wherewithal for a decent standard of living." He believed that "modern economists must devise a suitable means of price protection." Finally, he proclaimed that "in the plan of the Creator all of this world's goods are primarily intended for the worthy support of the entire human race."

Pope Paul VI usually addressed land issues in the context of world hunger or of the earth as intended by God for all. In his encyclical *Populorum Progressio (On the Progress of Peoples)* in 1967, he declared that every person has "the right to find in the world what is necessary for himself." Therefore, it must be stated that "private property does not constitute for anyone an absolute and unconditioned right. No one is justified in keeping for his exclusive use what he does not *need*, when others lack necessities" (emphasis added). Pope Paul thus reaffirms Aquinas' idea that people have an obligation to help others have at least life's necessities. He states that "the right to property must never be exercised to the detriment of the common good." Therefore, if those who have an abundance of land do not cultivate their property to aid other members of the human family, *expropriation* is an option for the state:

> If certain landed estates impede the general prosperity because they are extensive, unused or poorly used, or because they bring hardships to peoples or are detrimental to the interests of the country, the common good sometimes demands their expropriation (par. 24).

Pope Paul lamented the "ill-considered exploitation of nature" (*Octogesima Adveniens—The Eightieth Anniversary of Rerum Novarum,* 1971), and the exploitation of migrant workers. In his address to the World Food Conference in 1974, he proclaimed "No more hunger, hunger never again!"; noted that "aid to the agricultural sector has been notoriously insufficient"; stated that "there must be established a policy which will guarantee to the young people of rural areas the fundamental personal right to a deliberate choice of a worthwhile profession" fostered by governments "to give agriculture its rightful place"; taught that just as Jesus fed the hungry, so, too, must we heed Jesus' command, "Give them something to eat yourselves" (Matthew 14:16), through effective action; and declared:

> The right to satisfy one's hunger must finally be recognized for everyone. . . . This right is based on the fact that all the goods of the earth are destined primarily for universal use and for the subsistence of all men, before any individual appropriation (par. 5).

And in his "Bull of Indiction of the Holy Year 1975" (issued in 1974), Pope Paul spoke of the jubilee year and its prescriptions. He stated that the jubilee year "involved a new ordering of all things that were recognized as belonging to God: the land, which was allowed to lie fallow and was given back to its former owners, economic goods. . . ." For Pope Paul:

> The year of God, then, was also the year of Man, the year of the Earth, the year of the Poor, and upon this view of the whole of human reality there shone a new light which emanated from the clear recognition of the supreme dominion of God over the whole of creation (par. 34).

It was the Pope's hope that the Holy Year of 1975 would inspire people throughout the world to express a similar concern for the poor.

Probably no other Pope has addressed land issues as much as the current Pontiff, John Paul II. In his travels throughout the world, he has usually made it a point to address the rural constituency of the regions or nations that he visits. Several themes recur in his addresses, themes that relate back to the teachings of his predecessors. He declares that we must care for the land, that we are its stewards for the well-being of future generations as well as our own; he affirms the dignity and worth of all of the land's workers; he laments farmers' forced exodus to the city and the consequent exacerbation of urban problems; he urges farmers to organize to change their conditions; and he advocates changes in laws and structures so that a more just society can be developed. In his speech to the Indians of Oaxaca, Mexico, during his trip to the Latin American Bishops' Conference (CELAM III) in 1979, Pope John Paul stated that he was "with the mass of the population" and wanted to be "your voice, the voice of those who cannot speak or who are silenced." He then declared:

> Private property always carries with it a social mortgage, so that material possessions may serve the general goal that God intended. And if the common good requires it, there must be no doubt about expropriation itself, carried out in the proper manner.

He noted problems caused by the rural exodus to the city, problems such as "extended and painful unemployment and overcrowding of people in housing unworthy of human habitation." He urged farmers not to be individualistic "when it would be more helpful to act in a more coordinated and cooperative way." He declared that it was "not just" and "not Christian" for unjust situations to exist in which "powerful classes . . . keep the land unproductive and hide the bread which so many families lack." Later in 1979, Pope John Paul expanded his perspective on the land in his address to rural America, in Des Moines, Iowa. He stated that "the land is God's gift entrusted to people from the very beginning," and added that "the land is not only God's gift, it is also man's responsibility." He declared that "the land must be conserved with care since it is intended to be fruitful for generation upon generation," and said that if this were done "your children's children and generations after them will inherit an even richer land than was entrusted to you." He noted that farmers "cooperate with the Creator in the very sustenance of life on earth." He expanded on the idea of charity for the poor, stating that besides sharing food with the hungry, the agricultural community should also share "the knowledge we have gained" and promote "rural development everywhere," including rural work because "every person has a right to useful employment." The following year, 1980, Pope John Paul delivered rural addresses in Africa and Brazil. In Kisangani, Zaire, in rural Africa, he declared that rural people should not accept being considered "second-class men and women," because it would be neither just nor in conformity with the Gospel for "those who are strongest or most fortunate to exploit others." Again, he advocated "common actions" and a halt to the "rural exodus," and urged that Christians should be "concerned about the small and the weak," should "seek more just structures in the land area" and should "consider themselves managers of God's creation, which cannot be wasted or ravaged at will, for it is entrusted to men for the good of all."

In his homily in Recife, Brazil, a homily headlined in the Vatican newspaper *L'Osservatore Romano* as "The Land Is

God's Gift for All Men," Pope John Paul reiterated the same basic ideas. He stated that "the land is a gift of God, a gift that he makes to all human beings, men and women" and that therefore "it is not lawful, because it is not according to God's plan, to use this gift in such a way that its benefits are to the advantage of only a few, while the others, the vast majority, are excluded." He advocated "a just legislation in agricultural matters," noted that Christ is "on the side of the poor," called for "the indispensable transformation of the structures of economic life, always in favor of man" and consideration of "the living conditions of future generations" and, in words reminiscent to some extent of the American Indian concern for all of the world's creatures, declared that the earth "should be more and more in conformity with [God's] plans, the environment desired for all forms of life: the life of plants, the life of animals, and, above all, the life of men."

Pope John Paul, then, has consistently advocated a loving concern for the land and its inhabitants, and called for measures to promote their well-being.

VATICAN II

The individual voices of the bishops of Rome over the past score of years have been complemented by the collective voice of the bishops of the world gathered in council. In the Second Vatican Council, the bishops' document *Gaudium et Spes (Pastoral Constitution on the Church in the Modern World)*, issued in 1965, made several references to issues of property in general and land in particular, notably in paragraphs 66 through 71.

For the bishops, "God intended the earth and all that it contains for the use of every human being and people." Therefore, when a person uses possessions, that person should regard them not just as personal property, "but also as common property in the sense that they should accrue to the benefit not only of himself but of others." Everyone has "the right to have a share of earthly goods sufficient for oneself and one's family," and so people should share their goods with the poor. When this does not occur, "if a person is in extreme necessity, he has the right to take from the riches of others what he himself needs" (a direct reference to the teaching of St. Thomas Aquinas cited earlier). Goods are to be distributed not only as determined by present needs; they are to be so distributed as to provide "employment and sufficient income for the people of today *and of the future*" (emphasis added). The earth is the generational heritage of the human family.

The Council reiterates these ideas by stating that "by its very nature, private property has a social quality deriving from the law of the communal purpose of earthly goods." Government should "guard against any misuse of private property which injures the common good." What this might mean is that if "there are large or even gigantic rural estates which are only moderately cultivated or lie completely idle for the sake of profit," while simultaneously "the majority of the people are either without land or have only very small holdings, and there is evident and urgent need to increase land productivity," then "insufficiently cultivated estates should be distributed to those who can make these lands fruitful." The Council noted the special difficulties of farmers "in raising products or in selling them." It urged that they be helped "to obtain a fair return," lest they remain "lower-class citizens." Special attention also should be paid to migrants. In their case, "all discrimination with respect to wages and working conditions must be carefully avoided."

The teachings of the bishops at Vatican II clearly affirm this ethical principle, inherent in the Catholic tradition through the centuries: *property is social by nature.* All property, even manufactured property, is composed of parts of the earth which was created by God. The earth's fruits, even those harvested or formed by human hands, as well as the earth itself as land base, are all intended to serve the common good. No one has a right to selfishly hold for his or her *comfort* what others need for their *sustenance.* Property is not sacred, but the land is sacred, and the land's gifts are intended by God to satisfy the needs of *all* of God's creatures. Or, to put it another way, a person's private property is not sacred, but God's land is sacred, and we must "render to God the things that are God's."

In the particular context of the United States of America in the twentieth century, the Catholic Church's concern about matters of land ownership and use has emerged through organizations and individuals and, more recently, through national and regional bishops' statements.

In 1923, Edwin Vincent O'Hara, a priest of the diocese of St. Louis, Missouri (and later bishop of Kansas City, Missouri), organized the National Catholic Rural Life Conference. The NCRLC undertook such projects as rural Catholic education, organization of rural cooperatives and credit unions, and advocacy of land justice and stewardship. Throughout its history, spanning six decades, the NCRLC has been the longest-lived and, together with the urban-organized Catholic Worker movement, the most consistent Church advocate of land justice in the United States. The Conference's first permanent national office was established in St. Paul, Minnesota in 1934, and then was transferred to Des Moines, Iowa in 1941, where it remains today. It had its greatest impetus and expansion under the guidance of Monsignor Luigi Ligutti in the 1940's and 1950's. In his visit to rural America in 1979, Pope John Paul II commended "the dynamic and deserving Catholic Rural Life Conference."

The NCRLC has issued (or inspired the Church leadership to issue) numerous statements on land-related problems. In its *Manifesto on Rural Life*, a two hundred page statement promulgated in 1939, the NCRLC called for measures that would promote agrarian justice. The document also noted that "it would be a mistake to think that the problems of agrarianism are entirely rural," because what happens on the farm "has its repercussions in the city" and vice versa. The Manifesto states that "since God created the earth for mankind in general, the earth is the heritage of all mankind." In order for people to share in that heritage, "the right and opportunity to own property" is promoted and "the natural right to the fruits of labor" is advocated. The Manifesto notes that "while ownership of property is sacred and inviolable, it is not unlimited in the sense that a man may do with his property what he pleases without regard for the common good." Property, in other words, is seen as having a social obligation. This flows from the fact that in using property, an individual "is only exercising a stewardship" given by the Creator. This stewardship means further that "even in the absence of state regulations" the property must be administered "in the interests of the common good," and its use is "limited by the fundamental principles of social justice and social charity." This concept of ownership "avoids the extreme of individualism with its doctrine of absolute ownership and unlimited use." Private ownership, then, is advocated, but it is ownership as stewardship, ownership exercised on behalf of the common good. Moreover, "it follows that an economic system to be equitable must provide opportunity for the masses to become owners." Without such an opportunity, "the argument on which the right of private property rests is destroyed." Furthermore, "the stability of society requires widespread ownership."

In addition to, and often inspired by the National Catholic Rural Life Conference, individual bishops or bishops' committees or regions have advocated stewardship of God's land. Bishop George Speltz of St. Cloud, Minnesota, in his 1946 doctoral dissertation *The Importance of Rural Life* (published by the Catholic University of America Press), advocated "a wider distribution of property in land" with the understanding that "the right of the private owner is not absolute and must be interpreted in terms of the common good." The recommendations with which he concluded his work included that land be distributed to more farm families, that rural farm workers and urban workers have the opportunity to own and work the land, and that cities try to become more self-sufficient in the production of foodstuffs. In 1976 the Committee on Social Development and World Peace of the United States Catholic Conference issued a pamphlet entitled "Strip Mining: A Call for Regulation" which called for limitations on areas to be stripmined and advocated guidelines for their reclamation. In 1977 the "Statement of U.S. Catholic Bishops on American Indians" called for "the speedy and equitable resolution of treaty and statute questions" and the "protection of Indian land and resource rights." In 1979 the Committee on Social Development and World Peace issued "The Family Farm," calling for widespread farm ownership and stewardship of the land and its resources through reforms stimulated by "farmers themselves and the governments that set agricultural policy."

THE CATHOLIC WORKER MOVEMENT

During the time that the National Catholic Rural Life Conference and national bishops' committees were voicing their concern over land issues from a primarily rural perspective, a group of lay Church members from an urban center also advocated rural justice, but strongly coupled it to urban justice as well. From 1933 to the present, the Catholic Worker movement, originated by Dorothy Day and Peter Maurin, has proposed profound social reforms that include town and country unity. As part of its emphasis on the practice of the social ethical theory of the Catholic Church, the Catholic Worker movement advocated discussion sessions, "houses of hospitality" meeting the food, clothing, and shelter needs of the poor, and "agronomic universities." The latter were to be Catholic farming communes in which laborers and scholars would work together and exchange ideas on how to effect social justice. These "universities," part of a program of "cult, culture and cultivation," were to help bring about the harmonious relation of the earth and the earth's people. In its monthly newspaper, whose first number "was planned, written and edited in the kitchen of a tenement on Fifteenth Street, on subway platforms, on the 'L,' the ferry," in the heart of New York City, the Catholic Worker consistently addressed agrarian injustices, called on the government, the Church and especially individuals to work to eliminate them, and set up its own farming commune in Tivoli, New York (seventy miles from New York City) to practice the back-to-the-land part of its program and provide some of the food it distributed to the urban poor in its soup kitchen. Links with rural advocates of land justice are seen in some Worker issues. The November 1935 issue, for example, excerpted speeches of both Monsignor Ligutti and Bishop O'Hara from the National Catholic Rural Life Conference annual meeting. The main headline for the issue was "Back To Christ! Back To The Land!" and featured some of Peter Maurin's "Easy Essays" on the land. Maurin wrote, after advocating a society in which most people would practice agriculture:

> It is in fact impossible for any culture to be sound and healthy without a proper respect and proper regard for the soil, no matter how many urban dwellers think that their food comes from groceries and delicatessens or their milk from tin cans. This ignorance does not release them from a final dependence upon the farm. . . .
>
> The unemployed need free rent; they can have that on a farming commune. The unemployed need free food; they can raise that on a farming commune.

Maurin went on to state that the unemployed, professors and laborers, might find work and realize "worthy ideals" on a farming commune. In this urban-based organization called the Catholic Worker, then, an attempt is being made to sink rural roots in an effort to link the city and the country, serve the needs of the poor, get back in touch with the earth as the basic source of life, and, by these means, fulfill the social justice teachings of Jesus Christ.

From the Catholic bishops as individuals and in groups, and from concerned Catholic lay persons, the issues of land ownership and use have been discussed in ways parallel to the social encyclicals and speeches of the Popes. In another way, too, were these issues addressed: in the regional statements of bishops concerned about the implications of land justice for their particular area. Within the past few years, two such statements were promulgated by members of the Catholic hierarchy. *This Land Is Home to Me—A Pastoral Letter on Powerlessness in Appalachia* was issued in 1975, and *Strangers and Guests: Toward Community in the Heartland* was issued in 1980.

THIS LAND IS HOME TO ME

In 1973, a group of Appalachian Catholics concerned about the devastation of their region decided, at a Catholic Committee on Appalachia meeting, to formulate a statement on that concern. In conjunction with area bishops, they held a series of local and regional meetings. Then Joe Holland of the Center of Concern in Washington, D.C. wrote the final draft of the statement. Finally, on February 1, 1975, twenty-five bishops of the region signed *This Land Is Home to Me* at Wheeling College, West Virginia, during the Catholic Committee on Appalachia spring meeting. The title of the statement is derived from a song by Appalachia's Maureen Eaton.

The Appalachian bishops' land statement is an analysis of the social problems of the Appalachia region and their causes, and a vision of a better future for Appalachia with suggestions for steps that might be taken toward attaining it.

The bishops state that they are responding "to the cries of powerlessness from the region called Appalachia." They note that other voices with other views are heard in the region, but that "the poor are special in the eyes of the Lord." They see the struggles of the poor "in hollows," and "in industrial centers," and "in farmland." They observe that the saying "coal is king" is often heard in Appalachia because of the central role that coal plays in regional economics. People suffer when coal is mined because of their poor wages and working conditions; and people suffer when the mines close because then even the little they had is lost and they must migrate to the cities where "the people have to fight one another for a few jobs." The statement links regional exploitation with national affluence and international conflict, and calls the maximization of profit "a principle which too often converts itself into an idolatrous power." The earth's resources and human dignity alike are used up by that power: "profit and people frequently are contradictory," as Jesus indicated when he said that "no one can be the slave of two masters . . . you cannot be the slave both of God and money" (Matthew 6:24). Because "a country which took such richness from Appalachia left so little for the people" while "great fortunes were built on the exploitation of Appalachian workers and Appalachian resources," the people of Appalachia must struggle together—such as through "a strong and broad labor movement"—to change economic forces. The bishops declare that "economics is made by people," and so the people can change it. The bishops deplore the consumerism and adverse cultural influences that threaten to destroy the mountain people's dream of and struggle for justice.

The bishops state that God "is the God of the poor, because he frees the oppressed," and that the Church, although not perfect, continues "working for the poor, insisting on practical love, and not just prayers and good intentions." They place themselves squarely within the biblically-based Catholic social ethical tradition when they note that the bishops of an earlier era "called for a more just social order, where property would be broadly distributed and people would be truly responsible for one another," and when they state: "We must choose life. We must choose the living God." The bishops proclaim that "the goal which underlies our concern is fundamental in the justice struggle, namely, citizen control, or community control." It is essential for them that "the people themselves must shape their own destiny." In fact, the poor "must lead the way for all of us." The bishops call for the formulation of a comprehensive plan of action and the establishment of Centers of Reflection and Prayer and Centers of Popular Culture. They warn about "the presence of powerful multinational corporations" and suggest that "as a counterforce to the unaccountable power of these multinational corporations, there must arise a corresponding multinational labor movement, rooted in a vision of justice" that has a global concern for all workers, consumers and people in general. The bishops close with a challenge to the people "to be a part of the rebirth of utopias, to recover and defend the struggling dream of Appalachia itself," a dream "of simplicity and of justice."

The Appalachian bishops' land statement represented a significant step for the U.S. hierarchy. It was an effort to promote on a regional level and in a direct way the social teachings of the Catholic tradition, particularly those of the past century. It used examples directly pertinent to given historical circumstances instead of solely proclaiming incontrovertible but non-specific social principles. Its impact is still being felt as clergy, religious and laity in Appalachia, in their own concrete struggles for justice, use it, are strengthened by it, and are encouraged in their work by bishops who signed it.

STRANGERS AND GUESTS

As a direct consequence of *This Land Is Home to Me*, in 1978 a group of South Dakota farmers who were concerned about land consolidation and abuse in the midwest petitioned their own regional bishops to issue a land statement focusing on rural injustice in America's heartland. As a result, several meetings were held of an expanded group of midwestern farmers, priests, religious and bishops, particularly those active in the National Catholic Rural Life Conference whose president was then Bishop Maurice Dringman of Des Moines, Iowa. As a consequence of these meetings, the bishops of a twelve-state area (North Dakota, South Dakota, Minnesota, Wisconsin, Iowa, Kansas, Nebraska, Missouri, Indiana, Illinois, Colorado, and Wyoming) comprising forty-four dioceses decided to develop a land statement. The title for the document was taken from a verse in Leviticus 25:23, where God tells the Israelites that the land is his and that they dwell on it because of his goodness. After almost two years of public hearings were held on the statement, the bishops made their final amendments, and they issued *Strangers and Guests* on May 1, 1980. All of the region's sixty-seven active bishops, and five retired bishops, signed the document.

Strangers and Guests is similar to *This Land Is Home to Me* in that it analyzes social problems on the land in the light of the Scriptures and the Catholic tradition and proposes solutions for them. It is different in style, in its focus on the midwest from which it emerged, in its more formally developed land ethics, and in its broader authorship due to the larger number of people suggesting amendments to the bishops in its more widespread public hearings. *Strangers and Guests* is still ultimately, however, as was *This Land Is Home to Me,* a regional statement of the bishops who reflected on its various drafts, debated them and amended them, and finally appropriated the document as their own and affirmed its content by affixing their signatures to it. It represents the collective thinking on land issues of all the midwest's Catholic bishops.

The document begins with a Prologue expressing the bishops' concern about the events in the heartland: "We are witnessing profound and disturbing changes in rural America." These changes are the ways in which the land is being consolidated and abused, in contrast to earlier land stewardship practices. As the land suffers, so do the people who relate most closely to the land—family farmers, farmworkers, and Native Americans—and those who suffer most from the alteration of its production—the world's hungry. The document's three major sections then follow, discussing the midwest heritage in terms of land residency, ownership and use, Church teachings about the land, and ways to change land relations in the future.

The first part, "The Tenure of the Land," describes the ethnic, cultural, and social transformation of the heartland. The land was first inhabited by nomadic indigenous peoples who "shared an attitude of respect for the earth and for all the natural world," who had "a sense of harmony with nature and a sense of gratitude to the Spirit who provided for their needs through the bounty of the earth and other living creatures." But these Native Americans were forced from the land they once roamed freely and confined to reservations, and "property boundaries marked off land previously regarded as belonging to all and therefore to none." Farmers and ranchers came to occupy the land—but they, too, found out that more powerful speculators could subvert to their own purposes laws intended for the benefit of all. The land and the people suffered as profit-oriented interests gathered and abused large holdings of land. During this time, however, the structure of agriculture known as the family farm system did come into being:

> The family farm historically has been a moderate-sized farm the majority of whose land is owned, operated, managed and inhabited by members of the same family related by blood, marriage or adoption; a farm on which the majority of the labor is done by that same family; and a farm which provides a substantial part of the net income with which that family supports itself, an income adequate to meet that family's needs, ensure the survival of the farm, and provide some security for the future.

This description of the "family farm" was important for the whole of *Strangers and Guests,* because it portrayed a system that stood in marked contrast to trends in American agriculture. The bishops noted that such family farms have had a difficult time, especially in recent years because of the cost-price squeeze that farmers face. The cost of their land, machinery, seed, livestock, fertilizer, and other inputs, *a price not set by the farmer,* keeps rising; the price the farmer receives for agricultural products, *a price again not set by the farmer,* holds steady or declines or rises only slightly. The result is that farmers paying higher prices they cannot meet with their farm income are forced out of business. Many farmers complain bitterly about this squeeze, noting that they are the only group of people who go to the store to buy something—food, seed, implements, etc.—and must pay what the store owner asks, but then when they sell their own goods they must accept what others will give them. They have no means of setting a price on their own labor when confronted by government policies, corporate economic control, and agricultural exchanges such as the Chicago Board of Trade.

This first section of *Strangers and Guests* discusses other harmful land practices. The heartland region "rich in natural resources," benefits much more the nation in general and the corporations in particular than its own residents: mineral resources are extracted with little regard for social or environmental consequences. Forestry, too, has caused problems when timber extracted has not been replaced with seedlings and land has not been restored. Industrial pollutants plague land, water, air, and living creatures. Agricultural land is diverted for highways, suburbs and power plants and lines. The first part of the statement closes with the lament that "a sense of community has been lost" and a call for people "to reflect once again on our responsibility to be stewards of the land."

In the second part of *Strangers and Guests,* "Stewardship of the Land," a theological/ethical approach to land issues is proposed. With the Bible as base, ten "Principles of Land Stewardship" are offered:

1. The land is God's.
2. People are God's stewards on the land.
3. The land's benefits are for everyone.
4. The land should be distributed equitably.
5. The land should be conserved and restored.
6. Land use planning must consider social and environmental impacts.
7. Land use should be appropriate to land quality.
8. The land should provide a moderate livelihood.
9. The land's workers should be able to become the land's [civil] owners.
10. The land's mineral wealth should be shared.

These principles outline ways by which the earth might be distributed among its civil owners, respected and acknowledged as a trust from God. (In the original text, the word "civil" did not appear in the ninth principle. It is inserted here to avoid a contradiction between the first and ninth principles.)

1. The land is God's. This is the primary principle, the one from which all the others flow. God is the Creator, the One through whose love and will and word the earth and all it contains came into being. God still exercises dominion over the land as an interested, loving Presence guiding creation forward toward its Creator, prompting its evolutionary process and stages. Because "God created the earth, those living on it and the resources it provides," then we who have visible control over the earth must acknowledge that "to God's ultimate dominion all of these are subject."

2. People are God's stewards on the land. In the imagery of Genesis, God placed people in the garden of Eden "to cultivate and care for it" (2:15). Here we see God's mandate for all humanity: as Adam in the Genesis story is responsible and accountable for the garden, so, too, are we responsible and accountable for the land over which we have been given temporary dominion. We are to be *custodians* of the land and *conservers* of the land; we are to exercise human dominion over particular places in particular time periods according to particular social practices and civil law, yet still "subordinate to God's laws and the purpose for which God created the land"; and we are to care for our particular or social land holdings with "the best of current knowledge" of what will help them retain their vitality in order that the earth "might benefit present and future generations."

3. The land's benefits are for everyone. We who are stewards of the land, who have dominion over it in history, must recognize that "the land is given by God for all people, not just for those who hold civil title to it." All private—or collective—property in land is to be regarded as a "social mortgage," mortgaged from the whole of humanity while under the care of a part of humanity. "Private property is a good because of the benefits it confers on the many, not because of the advantages it gives to the few."

The land's benefits are for "everyone," and "everyone" does not just mean those who live today; it has transgenerational implications. This means that the land should not be self-ishly despoiled or severely depleted by any generation; the land is given by God "for present and future generations of humanity."

4. The land should be distributed equitably.   The essential idea expressed in this principle is that "land ownership should be as widely distributed as is necessary and feasible to meet the needs of the local and national communities and of the human family as a whole." This might mean, in some cases, widespread private (civil) ownership of the land, and, in other cases, ownership of the land by communities of people, such as those described in the Book of Acts in the New Testament: the members of the early Christian community who "shared all things in common" and divided everything "on the basis of each one's needs" (Acts 2:44–45). In any case, whether the land is owned *individually* by a great number of people, or *communally* by the people as a whole, it is always to benefit *all* of the people. The term "equitably," moreover, does not imply "equally" in the sense of everyone controlling land of the same size and agricultural quality; individuals' and families' needs, as well as land quality, must be taken into consideration.

5. The land should be conserved and restored.   The land which "is living and helps provide life for all creatures" must be cared for so that it will retain its regenerative power. In cases where "the subsurface resources of the earth have been extracted for human benefit, the land must be restored as nearly as possible to its original condition." By all of these means, the earth will not be allowed to be scarred and depleted, but rather will have its beauty and vitality preserved.

6. Land use planning must consider social and environmental impacts.   The land's characteristics were shaped by nature over millions of years and by humanity over a far lesser span of time. But people have in their power the means to alter in days what nature took eons to forge, and to adversely affect their own condition as well. When changes in an area are proposed, therefore, "land use planning must evaluate the impact that proposed courses of action would have" on the land

and people. Such impacts might affect health, jobs, community relations, natural beauty, and so forth. People, who are social beings and who have chosen to live and work in a particular place, should have "the principal right, where possible, to decide whether or not such changes should occur." This would imply once again that the rights of the fragile earth must also be considered; its internal integrity and its external role as the life source for the creatures living on it must be preserved.

7. Land use should be appropriate to land quality. The basic idea here is that the land should be developed or undisturbed depending on what is its "best and highest" use. What this means in practice is that because land is a limited resource susceptible to human alteration its use "should take into consideration the quality of the land and how it might best serve the community as a whole." For example, prime farmland, the world's best land for growing food, should not be paved over or stripmined. Both short- and long-term consequences of potential land uses should be evaluated when decisions are made about the disposition of the land.

8. The land should provide a moderate livelihood. The bishops state here that just as urban workers are entitled to what the Church has called a "living wage," so, too, rural workers should be able to derive from their labors on the land "sufficient money to provide for their needs and the needs of their family." Farmers, for example, should be able to meet their expenses and put aside some money for the future, just as urban workers do when they receive a living wage. The key word here is "moderate": the farm family is not to strive greedily to expand its holdings and wealth at the expense of near or distant neighbors in the human family; nor is the farm family to be impoverished by such things as a cheap food policy which keeps consumer prices low for food but forces farmers to struggle both against a social structure that penalizes their dedication and efficiency, and against the vagaries of nature. The farm family is to be neither wealthy nor poor, but moderately secure as it strives to meet its own basic needs and the food and fiber needs of the broader community.

9. The land's workers should be able to become the land's [civil] owners. Here the right is affirmed of agricultural, mining, forestry, and factory workers to "have some means of gradual entry into ownership of the land or corporation, either as individual owners or as shareholders." Those who work the land, who develop its resources, should be able by their labors to have a direct, civil proprietary relationship with and responsibility for that land. They have a right to become the land's stewards, as its civil owners; they are not to be locked into solely serving others' profit ventures.

10. The land's mineral wealth should be shared. Because "the mineral resources of our region are limited," and have profited corporations more than regional residents, the principle of sharing mineral wealth is proposed. The principle set forth here is not only a reaction against the exploitive extraction of iron, coal, gold, uranium, and other mineral resources in the heartland region, but also hearkens back to *This Land Is Home to Me,* where the Appalachian bishops lamented the loss of their region's rich coal resources and the concurrent impoverishment of their region's people. The exploitation of the land for corporate benefit and at community expense should not continue. Rather, boom and bust cycles should cease, and "the benefit which the people in the region derive from their natural resources should outlive the availability of those resources." Profits from mineral extraction should also "be shared in part by the people of the state in which mining occurs."

The third and final part of *Strangers and Guests,* "The Future of the Land," proposes remedies for the current crises in land ownership and use. The bishops pledge themselves to a "moral education" of the heartland and to acting to "effect legislative remedies if moral appeals for land stewardship do not alter the present situation." The bishops note that "governments as public bodies have the responsibility to mediate in a just manner the conflicting claims of the governed." Among the types of government intervention might be: limiting "the rights of individual investors and of investor-owned companies to acquire land"; elimination of capital gains tax laws which favor "wealthy investors and land speculators" and disfavor "small and low income farm families"; taxation of agricultural land "according to its productive value rather than according to its speculative value"; enforcement of mining laws and the use of severance taxes to restore exploited areas and provide for rural community needs; encouragement of urban inner development rather than external expansion onto agricultural land; encouragement of modest-sized land holdings "by taxing land progressively at a higher rate according to increases in the size and quality of holdings" (a proposal in the Jeffersonian tradition!); stabilization of agricultural prices; low interest loans to aspiring farmers and tax incentives for other farmers to sell land to them; renunciation of the use of food as an oppressive weapon, because food should never be used "against any nation or people as a tool of oppression to starve them into submission"; preservation of land and water resources through such means as agricultural zoning; promotion of conservation practices; review of seed patent laws; "just wages and reasonably healthy working conditions" for farmworkers, miners and timber workers; and resolution of American Indian treaty disputes and protection of American Indian rights to land and its resources. The agenda for government action is long—but so is the list of abuses to which the midwestern bishops respond.

Strangers and Guests is, at this writing, the most recent Catholic bishops' regional land statement. Regional Catholic bishops' responses to land issues might continue, however, if Church leaders in other areas address questions of land justice from their own context.

VOICES FROM OTHER TRADITIONS

The work of the Catholic Church does not stand alone; several other Christian denominations have issued strong statements about land stewardship implications.

The United Church of Christ, for example, issued a pro-

nouncement at its 1979 General Synod: "Rural America: Life
and Issues." This four-part document included policy statements which declared, in part, that there should be a minimal
"diversion of agricultural land to non-food producing uses"; a
"careful examination of the use of eminent domain"; a federal
government policy that would "respect the land and water
rights of all peoples, especially minorities and those guaran-
teed in Native American treaties"; the "development of de-
centralized energy technologies including alternative energy
sources"; an acknowledgement that rural workers have the
right "to organize and to engage in collective bargaining"; and
a national policy to preserve and strengthen the family farm,
complemented by state legislation "prohibiting or limiting the
ownership and operating of farms by large non-family corporations." This church pronouncement contains other provisions
which also complement the courses of action advocated in
Strangers and Guests.

The United Presbyterian Church in the U.S.A. also issued
a statement on land issues, focusing on agriculture. This policy
statement, "The Family Farm," was promulgated at the
church's 1978 General Assembly. The document urges scruti-
ny of farm-related tax laws and their modification, as necessary, "to avoid giving greater benefits to the large-scale farm
operations"; careful land use planning that would "protect
farm land from indiscriminate diversion to non-farm uses"; a
legal ban on "applications of fertilizers and pesticides in excess
of amounts needed that jeopardize soil, waterways and food
supplies"; the enactment of legislation which "limits or prohib-
its farm ownership or farm operation by large-scale non-family
corporations"; enforcement of federal anti-trust laws "in the
food and agricultural sector"; "increasing minority farm ownership"; and "organized market bargaining efforts by groups of
farmers." In these and other proposals of the statement, a careful and caring stewardship of agricultural lands is advocated by
the Presbyterian Church representatives.

Some of the strongest pronouncements about land issues
have come from the Lutheran Church in America. Two of its
"Social Statements" in particular are clarion calls for care of

the land. In a 1972 statement entitled "The Human Crisis in Ecology" we are taught:

> God so orders creation that everything in it is related to everything else. . . . When any part is tampered with, exploited or destroyed, the effect is felt in other parts and eventually in the whole system. The ecological crisis consists in the radical violation of the systems God creates.

The statement deplores the "pollution of air, water, soil, and sound" and urges the adoption of "new values which give priority to quality of life rather than to quantity of things." The document declares: "Human beings are part of the vast ecosystem of the planet earth. They cannot live their lives against that system; they must live within it," and it calls for the "development of ecological life styles which are sensitive to the needs of human beings and the non-human world." This Lutheran statement on land use is complemented by one entitled "Economic Justice—Stewardship of Creation in Human Community," in which property rights are discussed. The church declares that "the holder of [private] property may not assert exclusive claim on it or its fruits":

> Private property is not an absolute human right but is always conditioned by the will of God and the needs of the community. The obligation to serve justifies the right to possess. The Creator does not sanction the accumulation of economic power and possessions as ends in themselves.

In these two statements we see once again how another church within the Christian tradition, drawing on the same biblical base as its sister Christian churches, advocates respect for and justice on the land. Similar sentiments are expressed in such other church writings as *And He Had Compassion on Them: The Christian and World Hunger* and *For My Neighbor's Good,* two study guides from the Christian Reformed Church; "The Christian Rural Mission In The 1980's—A Call to Liberation and Development of Peoples," from the Agricultural Missions of the National Council of Churches; an ecumenical "Interfaith Statement on Public Policy and the Structure of Agriculture," presented to the USDA: and the study resource "The Family Farm: Can It Be Saved?" from the United Methodist Church. In all of these documents, the Christian churches express concern over land consolidation and abuse and the impact of changes in land tenure and use on human needs, especially the needs of the hungry.

WHY THE CHURCH?

As the Catholic Church and other Christian denominations have become involved in land issues, proponents of the status quo, those who have a stake in the continued exploitation of the land, often question Church involvement in social issues. The Church is accused of becoming "too political" and of "not sticking to the Gospel." Such a point of view passes over the possibility that Church silence might also be seen as political, as an acceptance or affirmation of the way things are. It also represents a limited acceptance of the Gospel, and therefore a distortion of the message of Jesus.

In the New Testament we are taught, and we who are baptized profess as part of our faith, that Jesus is God incarnate, God among us, God enfleshed. Rather than teach us by a vision or by internal inspiration, God chose to come among us as one of us. In this way, the worth of the creation that flowed from God was affirmed, and any effort to deny the goodness of the created world—"God saw that it was good"—is negated. Similarly, people are reconfirmed as God's stewards on the land, and they are responsible for each other as well. Jesus instructs us to "feed the hungry," to "give drink to the thirsty" and to "clothe the naked." If we are driven from the land, or have no control over what it produces or to whom its produce is distributed, how could we fulfill the Lord's command? The Church is in the world as the ongoing bearer of the "good news"—the Gospel—of salvation from sin on all its levels, the social and political as well as the personal and private. The

Church, the people of God, the community of believers, must witness to God's love for the world God created and entrusted to us—we who are God's images and stewards.

Through all of the statements and speeches and essays emanating from Church people, some common reflections thread their way: a recognition of God's sovereignty over God's creation, a realization of human stewardship responsibilities, and a reclamation of principles of land justice that include civil land ownership in the interest of all peoples and land use in the interest of the well-being of the earth and all its inhabitants. The Church must integrate these reflections into its *individualized* concern for the whole *person*, body and spirit, personal and social, and into its *global* concern for the whole *family* of humanity, people of every race, creed, social class, sex, culture, and nation. Such a holistic view of the needs of the land and its people will help promote justice on the land and for the land. One of the ways by which that justice will be promoted is through the intervention of a government prodded into helping the landless obtain land through expropriation and redistribution of existing large estates, through revision of tax structures benefiting the wealthy, through bettering the wages and working conditions of the land's laborers. Another way would be through individuals' acceptance of the principles of land justice, and their consequent efforts to put them into practice both in their individual lives and in the wider community and nation through land-interested organizations. Finally, in all these efforts, an understanding should exist of the common family bond that unites all peoples of all generations. The hungry must be fed—tomorrow as well as today. Thus the land must be worked to help meet their needs today and be conserved to meet their needs tomorrow; and to better enable it to meet their needs tomorrow, its ownership must be widespread or communal (whichever best serves humanity in a given place and time), and agricultural knowledge, techniques, and technology must be shared. The consistent theme in all of these efforts should be this: The land is entrusted by God to people who are to care for it and facilitate the just distribution of its fruits.

TRADITION, HERITAGE, AND THE STRUGGLE
FOR THE FUTURE

Some major points of convergence occur between the Church's tradition and the American heritage described previously. Essentially, both perspectives believe that the land is a community heritage, that its civil ownership privileges and fruits should be distributed in the community interest, that it should be cared for as a community benefit and that, where necessary, government must intervene as community in the interest of community to ensure the common good in questions of land ownership and use. Because of this convergence, a common philosophy and common interest exist for American—Native American and immigrant American—people of religious conviction to build on this historical base a political and economic structure that embodies the best of the ethical theory of justice on the land. The underlying philosophy of justice will conflict, in its practical manifestations, with some prevailing attitudes and practices. But if the American dream of justice for all and the Christian vision of a new person in a new society are to be realized, the conflict must be accepted and the struggle begun. The needs of the "least of Jesus' brethren" require nothing less. The struggle for the future is a struggle in the present to determine if the struggles of the past have or have not been in vain. The struggle for the future is the struggle to continue into the future, a movement toward a just society, on justly distributed land, sharing justly distributed fruits of the land. Without a struggle for the future, the people of the land will lose continually their sense of their own history, their freedom in their present, and their control over their own destiny. In contrast, if the call of the future is answered, and commitment to its better possibilities is evidenced by a struggle for its realization, then the dreams of the American heritage and the visions of the religious traditions will be ever more closely approximated.

chapter six

Land Reform

*   *   *

The scenes that we have seen of devastated or consolidated land contrast sharply with the visions of a beautiful, bountiful and shared earth that are presented to us in our religious and national traditions. As we contemplate this disparity between reality and vision, we might wonder what we might do in order that they might become congruent.

In a variety of ways, what our current context requires is *land reform.* For many, the latter term or the concept of practices it represents provokes alarm or anger: because of the path that land reform has taken in other countries they fear for their property or for a loss of social stability. In the light of our previous discussions of abuses of the land, and of our hope for a better future for the land and its inhabitants, however, we might thoughtfully reflect on just what might be meant by "land reform" in our nation's context. In order to do that , we should consider both what is meant by "form" and what is then implied by "reform."

First of all, form can mean *structure,* the systematic way something is put together. The form of land relations in our nation, for example, is primarily individual ownership, ownership of the land as exclusive property. The structure rules the relations among individuals such that you and I know that this is *my* property and that is *your* property. Each of us knows that we have the civil right to hold onto our own property and exclude others from it: they have no right to what is ours.

Second, form can mean *shape*, the appearance of something, how it is being used. The form of the land as shape is determined primarily by what the ones who control the land (usually the owners) decide to do or not to do with land shaped by nature or by previous inhabitants. Generally, none of us questions how others use their land. They might decide to preserve a wilderness or conserve prime agricultural land—or they might decide to convert either or both into suburban housing or a strip mine. The form of the land has the possibility of natural or ordered beauty, or disordered exploitation. Except in rare cases of government use of eminent domain, overriding the individual in favor of the community (often exercised, unfortunately, on behalf of powerful individuals or corporations covetous of the lands of the powerless or seemingly powerless), we usually tend to let others use their land as they see fit (unless, for example, their lack of conservation practices creates erosion of my soil, or their allowance of indiscriminate toxic chemical waste dumping or uranium mining imperils the health of ourselves or our families). We do not ordinarily question how others shape their land.

Third, form can mean *social setting*, the way in which structures and shapes interrelate. If individual license is unrestrained or hardly restrained by the broader society, then the form of the land's social setting is one of control of the many by the few with consequent civil strife or, at the least, social unrest. When people have no land base and suffer, while seeing others prosper on their property, then they question at least the particular aspect of the social setting called property relations. We have seen how indigenous peoples believed in sharing, not owning, the land; we have seen, too, how the founders of the American republic tried to set forth a theory of equitable rights on the land, and how their perspective lived on in the speeches, writings and actions of later Americans; and we have seen also that the Christian ethical tradition affirms the principles of equitable ownership and community of use. As landless people reflect on any or all of these parts of our American heritage, they cannot but question a social setting that denies them that heritage. It is in the social setting, then, that the structure of the land and the shape of the land are questioned, and the call for reform emerges.

If those are the forms of the land, what, then, might be meant by "land reform"?

Land reform means land *re-form:* changing the current forms taken on or by the land in order to create new forms more consonant with the principles transferred through the centuries. There must be a *re-form of ownership:* that is, the structure of land relations must be so altered as to permit a more widespread civil ownership of the land by individuals or communities of people. There must be a *re-form of use:* that is, the shape of the land must be conserved or ordered in accordance with the needs of the earth community. There must be, finally, a *re-form of relationships:* new or alternative relationships must be formulated so that the vision of justice expressed and hoped for in national and religious traditions might become the new social reality. Land re-form means, in summary, alteration of property relationships, ecological relationships and social relationships, all with the intention of promoting and effecting the congruence of human conduct and the ethical vision of the highest possibility for that conduct, relative to life in the earth community.

In order that we might bring about land reform our social vision and social context must help us to live a social conduct that catalyzes change. What is needed is *transformational ethics,* that is, ethics for changing our social context so that it might conflate with our social vision. The basis for that social ethics of transformation applied to the earth would be principles of land relations summed up as follows: the land is God's; the land is entrusted to humanity; and the land is to be shared equitably through the ages. What we need to do now is to reflect on (then act on) practical ways of practicing transformational ethics, ways of transforming our presently unethical land attitudes and practices into closer approximations of our understanding and our vision of what should be and could be. Were we to put our transformational ethics into practice, we might take the twenty steps that follow. They show what a Christian should do about injustices in land ownership, land use and distribution of the land's fruits. They are practicable by urban or rural dwellers acting as individuals or groups, independently or conjointly.

TWENTY STEPS OF LAND REFORM

The following steps are not intended to be undertaken in any particular order (except for the first three). They are meant as guides as to how Christians as individuals or as a group might respond to the issues raised in this book and in their own area. The steps might have greater or lesser applicability or feasibility, depending on the personal circumstances and social context of the one(s) considering undertaking them.

1. Take a ride or a walk through as many of the following as is possible: rural backroads, inner city streets, an Indian reservation, a stripmine area, a national or state park. *Analyze their present condition*: Is the land treated with respect? Is it utilized according to its best and highest use? Does its civil ownership structure reflect few or many property holders? Are public lands cared for as a public trust, or are they primarily benefiting private individuals? Are the people living there owners? Are the people working there owners? Think over your answers to those questions.

2. *Learn and reflect on* our biblical roots, our Christian tradition and our American heritage, to regain the sense of justice in land relations that weaves its way through them and makes of them complementary perspectives. Does their understanding about the land complement or contradict what we have learned about property and land from our family, our educational system, our church, our media, our friends and our associates? What are the reasons for points of conflict? On which side do we place ourselves, and why?

3. Find a place of solitude and *meditate on the immanence of God.* We are accustomed to seeing God as transcendent, but we must also see God as immanent to better understand ourselves and our world, and our responsibilities as temples and images of a God immanent in creation. Try to ex-

perience God within. Then go and see if you can recognize God in other people, in plants and trees, in rivers and rocks, in birds and fish and animals. This experience will bring a sense of the earth community, of how we all live in God and are responsible to God—and so for each other, according to who we are as creatures of God. Reflect on what you have seen and heard, outside of you and in you. Share your reflections with others: family, friends, church members, teachers, students, business associates. Encourage them to do as you have done.

4. Fortified with the understanding that you have from your analysis, knowledge, communication with others and experience of God's presence, **promote that understanding in the broader community.** Reflect on the next steps to see which of them *you* might take to promote an active concern for the earth community, one that is expressed in actions aimed at making the natural and social environment more congruent with what you have come to realize *should* be. Do not be overwhelmed by the task: it is not "all or nothing." God gives each of us different roles and we have our individual abilities, experiences, strengths and weaknesses. God will guide and support us as we *are* and help us, too, to become more who we *should be.* Keeping that in mind, consider the steps that follow. They indicate personal lifestyle changes as well as social action.

5. If you have land of your own, **order your environment,** even if you have just a backyard. Plant a vegetable garden and, if space and climate permit, fruit and nut trees. In this way, you will have a home grown, naturally healthier, less expensive food supply to meet some of your nutritional needs. More important, you will experience a sense of communion with the earth as you work with its rhythms, its soil, its nutrients, and the living plants that you co-create with it, its elements and the sun's energy. You will understand a great deal more about this community called earth, about its ecological interrelatedness and balance. You will understand directly what it means to steward the earth, to be a trustee of the land. You will feel the part of nature that you are, and understand how human ordering of nature is a natural process because we, too, are part of

nature. As you work with the land, try to use solely *organic* gardening methods: the food will be healthier and safer and the soil will be conserved and enriched and underground and surface water supplies will not be affected by chemical contamination (for tips on organic gardening methods, consult issues of *Organic Gardening* and *Mother Earth News* magazines, and books from Rodale Press). Try also to plant shade trees around your home in order to decrease your energy consumption and costs and lessen depletion of energy reserves: it is an individual or familial way of helping to save the land from being diverted to less appropriate uses. Plant flowers, too, around your home (or tend flowers and plants in your home or apartment) to experience their beauty, satisfy mutual and complementary needs (for them, life, growth and survival, depending on your care; for you, being in touch with the earth and, also, enjoying its colorful or soothing green beauty), and enhance your home, your place on the land.

If you have little or no land, explore with family, friends, and neighbors the possibility of a community garden on a vacant lot or lots. Such a community garden provides many of the same benefits as a home garden and an additional one: sharing with others the experience of working the land. This sharing helps cement bonds of community in the human family, and promotes communication of the experience of touching and working the land. One example of community-type gardens in operation is the youth garden program active for several decades in the Cleveland school system. In this community effort, youths learn gardening, experience the earth and develop discipline and industriousness. In 1974, the 21,000 participant young people grew a conservatively estimated $622,000 worth of home grown vegetables.

You might also work in community efforts to order the environment by promoting and working on communally—or co-operatively—owned agricultural land. This experience promotes an even greater awareness that God is the land's ultimate owner, that we are its stewards and trustees, and that its fruits are community benefits. The spirit of the community here would be similar to that of the early Christian community described in Acts 4:32–35:

> The community of believers were of one heart and one mind. None of them ever claimed anything as his own; rather, everything was held in common. With power the apostles bore witness to the resurrection of the Lord Jesus, and great respect was paid to them all; nor was there anyone needy among them, for all who owned property or houses sold them and donated the proceeds. They used to lay them at the feet of the apostles to be distributed to everyone according to his need.

Common ownership of property in land can express, then, acceptance of the role of trustee of the land and a concomitant commitment to serve the needs of the landless poor.

Finally, you might promote family farm agriculture in your own area by selling your own farm land—or, if you have none, by encouraging others to sell their farm land—to aspiring farmers or small family farmers rather than just to the highest bidder (who might be a large-scale operator; a doctor only investing money, not time and effort and care, into the land to make a profit from it; a representative of a profit-oriented land management company aiding wealthy investors; or a buyer for foreign interests). You might also encourage your local and national government officials to devise tax incentives for that practice so that families that are financially burdened would be able to make such a choice.

6. Utilize **energy conservation techniques** around your home. When renovating or constructing a home, see where you might utilize solar heating, cooling and hot water systems. These might be *passive* (using sun, shade, wind currents and earth berms) or *active* (using mechanical assistance). Also consider using wind power, where local laws and codes permit, for partial or total provision of electricity (depending on your consumption): some highly efficient windmill systems require wind of only three to four miles per hour to generate electrical

power. Here again, energy expenses will be diminished over time and less demands will have to be made on the environment for mining and for construction of power plants and lines. The perceived "need" for harmful nuclear power would be eliminated as well, enabling a healthier environment to exist.

As a corollary, construct a solar cold frame to provide home grown vegetables through the winter, even in the coldest climates. This use of solar technology would enable you to keep in touch with the earth's life-regenerative process through the period when plant life is dormant, and also decreases in some small way your dependence for food on canneries and distant producers, thereby promoting again some savings in depletion of the earth's mineral and fuel resources.

7. *Form or join a local food co-op.* Such cooperatives, which multiplied in the 1960's with a heightened interest in community living and sharing and vegetarian diet, enable their members to purchase food at less than supermarket prices—and, frequently, at better than supermarket quality. Food co-ops, also, to some extent, allow members to bypass the control of the large market corporations. In addition, they have helped poor people—including the elderly—to purchase nutritious foods that they would not otherwise have been able to afford.

Corollary activities to a co-op would be organization of *gleaning* opportunities for the poor and elderly, and provision of food to them and the unemployed and their families in Catholic Worker-type *houses of hospitality.*

In the first instance, people would be allowed by farmers and agribusinesses to pick leftover produce after the harvest is done. Food that would otherwise go to waste can thus provide sustenance for the hungry, who have the added benefit (when they are physically able) of working with the earth when it is yielding its fruits.

In the second instance, food that has been begged, donated or gleaned would be prepared for consumption by the downtrodden hungry once or twice daily. Soup lines, served by members of a church or civic organization, would be a dramatic and direct means of seeing and responding to Jesus in the least of our brethren: "For I was hungry and you . . ."

8. Establish a *farm-to-market program* at your church. This is especially beneficial for urban areas where no sustained contact with the land or with people of the land occurs. Urban residents and farmers would have the opportunity to meet and, optimally, discuss their problems and come to understand each other better. People of the city would also be able to have fresh vegetables of a better price and quality than available in stores. Such arrangements also provide support for local family farmers whose produce is often not purchased by chain supermarkets that frequently prefer buying larger quantities from agribusiness corporations sometimes located in distant areas. Support of local farmers means support also for family farm agriculture and for conserving energy supplies that are consumed by cross-country produce trucks and trains.

9. Evaluate your *family's food and energy consumption* patterns. How balanced is your diet? Are you consuming too much salt, or too much sugar (in the latter case, forcing domestic workers to labor in difficult conditions for inadequate pay, and foreign workers and farmers to utilize agricultural land for your pleasure rather than their needs), or too much meat (which is sometimes from domestic animals that have high levels of drugs, or from foreign animals whose production diverted land, again, from meeting basic food needs)? What foods shipped from afar might you give up in order to help foreign workers or domestic energy conservation? What energy conservation measures do you use at home? If you smoke, how will you begin *today* to wean yourself from a habit that poisons you and members of your family (especially the most susceptible youngest members) and is based on a crop—tobacco—that deprives the soil of its nutrients and displaces food crops from valuable agricultural land? These questions might seem pointed and difficult—but so are the problems that generate them, problems that will be resolved only when people answer them with the interests of the earth community at heart.

10. Participate in *land justice-oriented organizations* such as the National Catholic Rural Life Conference (head-

quartered in Des Moines, Iowa, and open to any land-interested person) or a similar group studying and acting on land issues. Attend farmer organization meetings where possible, whether you are a farmer or not. If you are a family farmer, your best hope for economic survival lies in participation in the organized efforts of farm organizations. If you are a city dweller, your initial contact with family farmers and beginning efforts at understanding their problems might well be a farm meeting. Establish or join local church-based chapters of land- and food-oriented groups such as the National Catholic Rural Life Conference, Bread for the World, Rural America and others.

11. *Protest national misuse of food* to your U.S. senators and representatives. Particularly, express your dissatisfaction with inadequate nutrition programs for the poor and elderly, and with any suggested use of food as a weapon, a threat or promotion of starvation of a nation or people in disagreement with U.S. government and business policies and practices. Mindful that the earth's fruits are intended for all the people of every generation, press for a comprehensive international food policy that takes into account the resources of the agriculturally rich nations and the hunger that plagues some of their own people as well as those in poorer nations. Protest against seed patent laws that promote agricultural production and marketing monopolies and put the power of control over the world's food supply into a few hands.

12. Advocate *changes in the capital gains provisions of tax laws,* since these provisions encourage non-operator investment in agriculture and inflated bidding for available land at prices beyond the reach of aspiring family farmers or small family farmers. The family farm system of agriculture eventually will no longer be a part of American agriculture if the economic incentive for agricultural investment is not taken away. Many small farmers themselves do not recognize that capital gains tax incentives, while benefiting them only in the short-term, benefit large operators to a far greater extent in both the short- and long-term. Urban investors must also recognize that they are hurting family farmers and the future of the land

when they seek short-term profits from agricultural land. Changes in the tax provisions could be a disincentive for agricultural speculation and an incentive for owner-operator-resident family farms.

13. Promote the formation of local *agricultural districts or agricultural zoning* to preserve prime farm land from diversion away from its best and highest use—agriculture— through speculation and urban-related development. Encourage soil conservation stewardship on agriculturally zoned land, so that its agricultural use may be sustained. If you are a landholder, try to support such districts or zones, even if you might incur some financial loss when selling your property, in the interest of the needs of the human family and of the land that nourishes it.

14. Support *minority group efforts to obtain or keep a land base.* Such support might be financial, through contributions to minority organizations; verbal, through conversations with friends and associates, and letters to the editor or to members of your congressional delegation (since much minority-related legislation is passed at the federal level); physical, through your presence at meetings, marches, rallies and workshops. Minority groups, such as southern black farmers, American Indian nations, Appalachian small farmers, Chicano and other ethnic migrant farm workers and women seeking entry into agriculture on their own—members of all of these groups are struggling to retain or obtain their own land on which to live and work. In some areas, they might be a numerical majority but an economic minority, and so are powerless to fight the wealthy, gain access to the media, or oppose corrupt political processes. And while they are engaged in the struggle for land of their own, support their efforts to obtain better wages (for justice's sake, as well as to enable them eventually to purchase land and leave the poverty cycle) and working conditions (for justice's sake, as well as to enable them to be healthy for their present work for others and their future work for themselves and their families).

15. Promote a *progressive land tax,* along Jeffersonian lines, a tax graduated according to the size and quality of hold-

ings and specific within each state according to what is needed in a given area for a farm family to have a just measure of economic self-sufficiency. Within such a tax structure (similar in operation to our progressive income tax, but without tax breaks for the well-to-do), a tax-free homestead exemption could apply to about ten acres (depending on the type of farm, the quality and price of land and other local factors) upon which the farmhouse is located, and then a graduated rate by designated amounts of acres on the rest of the land, so that large holdings would be discouraged as economically unfeasible, and large farms broken up and redistributed in smaller sizes to aspiring farmers and small family farmers. (For an analysis of how tax laws adversely affect family farmers and benefit agribusiness, see agricultural economist Harold Breinmeyer's book, *Farm Policy: 13 Essays*, published by the Iowa State University Press.)

Another possibility for a land tax, in conjunction with the progressive land tax, might be some development and application of the single tax idea of Henry George: taxation of the land, not its improvements, so that people would be encouraged either to improve their land to make a profit from it, or to sell it to others. Were such a tax to be developed, it should make provision for the best and highest use of land (for example, farm land taxed at a lower rate, to promote family farm survival; scenic land taxed at a lower rate—or not at all, if used as a public benefit—to ensure non-exploitation of natural beauty and of wildlife habitats), and for the needs of the human family in particular and the earth community in general (for example, exemptions for community gardens or farms, and taxation at a lower than mineral rate for agricultural land or scenic land or home-occupied land that contains subsurface coal or uranium, as long as mineral extraction does not take place or, taking place, alters the surface very little).

16. Promote a *progressive estate tax,* similar in structure to the progressive land tax, with the intent of neither forcing family farmers from the land when a head of household dies and the taxes on inflated land and capital values exceed the family's ability to pay and require sale of the family farm, nor

of allowing the building of *terracracy*, a landed aristocracy whose holdings keep increasing with succeeding generations. It was to prevent the latter that Jefferson and other revolutionary leaders proposed an estate tax in the first place; it is to prevent the former, which was not the intent of estate tax legislation, that the tax should be progressive. Again, the tax should be so structured that both possibilities would be prevented or diminished. This might require that some family farms, the largest ones, decrease in size as the estate is passed on. But the overall intent, again, is that moderate-sized family farms result, so that such farms may be operated by heirs or other aspiring or small farmers. This tax, too, should have a homestead exemption and should be higher on non-owner operated and uninhabited holdings.

17. Support *farm prices closer to parity,* so that farmers may emerge from the cost-price squeeze that, together with high interest rates and government indifference, is forcing them off the land. Support for parity should be qualified, however, with some link to the progressive taxes cited previously, and some requirements for soil conservation practices and decreased agricultural dependency on chemical fertilizers, herbicides, and pesticides. If farmers are going to receive higher prices, then they need not overwork and deplete the earth as many are now doing in their struggle for survival or their greed for high profits. Parity is a good only when the community as a whole benefits from its application, not when it just assures farmers economic benefit and family and job security and prosperity. As a corollary to parity, import quotas and taxes on agricultural products should be imposed or strengthened. This would prevent unfair economic competition from international marketing by other countries or transnational corporations, pressure other countries to devote their agricultural resources to feed their own people and to sell to poorer nations at lower prices, and inhibit the flight of U.S. corporations to foreign nations to exploit land and people so as to sell agricultural goods back to the U.S. for corporate profit, to the detriment of foreign and U.S. farmers, farm workers and consumers. If the concept of parity is difficult for urban workers

and consumers to accept because of the job and financial security it provides for farmers and because of the potential for higher food prices in the supermarket, the alternative should be kept in mind: a U.S.—and world—agricultural system owned and controlled by a handful of corporations with profit, not land or people, as their primary concern, with a consequent overworking of the land, chemical poisoning of it (and so of the food grown on it), provision of less nutritious and more tasteless food (remember those hard, square tomatoes developed for picking and shipping, not nutrition and taste), and higher prices extorted from the public for monopolized agricultural products.

18. Advocate *enforcement of laws conserving the land,* such as the 1902 Reclamation Act (just recently diluted in part by congressional submission to corporate pressures to increase the amount of land irrigated at taxpayer's cost from one hundred and sixty acres to nine hundred and sixty acres per person—which will still be subverted by the corporation); the Federal Surface Mining Control and Reclamation Act of 1977; laws setting aside and preserving national and state parks, forests and seashores; severance tax laws that have the impact not only of providing local or state revenue for local or state mineral products, but also tend to make corporations less reckless and exploitive in mining, drilling and stockpiling natural resources that belong ultimately to God and, by God's beneficence, to the whole human family; soil conservation laws that restrict land abuse and provide funds for such conservation measures as terraces and windbreaks; and laws imposing a freeze on, and promoting the reduction and eventual elimination of, nuclear weapons that threaten all the earth.

19. Promote *regional ownership of energy resources* (by state or group of states)—oil, natural gas, coal, uranium, geothermal, hydro—and of their development, production and distribution. These resources, again, are intended to benefit all of us, and not to provide huge profits for oil and coal corporations so that they might control our economy, purchase and restrict solar development companies and techniques, and buy control of non-energy-related enterprises (such as farm lands,

food companies, catalogue sales companies, and so on). This regional ownership should be coordinated on a national level by the federal government. A certain balance of powers is essential here. If the federal government were sole owner and controller (as the state is in a communist or socialist nation), too much power would be given to too few people. If the regional body were sole owner and controller, a local monopoly based on greed and unconcern for others might prevent a national (and global) sharing of public resources (one might recall here the reluctance of such energy-rich areas as the west to share their reserves, at a reasonable price, with northeastern families and factories during recent severe winters; or midwestern and southwestern cries of "Let them go bankrupt!" when New York City—through which most Americans' ancestors passed and profited from as immigrants—was in financial difficulty; or OPEC—Organization of Petroleum Exporting Countries—control of oil resources that could reach extortion levels, harming poor nations as well as heavily industrialized nations, although, of course, this does not deny that OPEC countries have been exploited economically and politically by Western industrial powers' governments and corporations, and that those same wealthy nations need to practice much greater energy conservation). The federal government (the national public) and the regional energy corporation (the regional public) would work cooperatively in the public interest in the development and distribution of energy resources.

20. If you have the requisite ability, commitment and financial resources, *campaign for public office*—city, county, state, national—to promote the principles of land reform stated in this chapter. This land advocacy would occur during your campaign as you raise fundamental land and food issues, and, should you be successful, during your tenure in office as you propose and fight for policies that will promote necessary changes in land ownership patterns and land use practices. If you are unable to be a candidate yourself, then evaluate carefully those who do aspire to attain or retain public office and work with those having a stewardship perspective on the land and its resources. The land issue is a most fundamental issue,

for we depend on the earth's resources for the food, fiber, shelter, water and energy that we need as individuals and community for our very survival. A word of caution, however: to work for stewardship of the land is to risk being called a "communist" in our U.S. society, for when you base your actions on fundamental biblical principles and commands, you enter into conflict with the prevailing American atheist ideology of "survival of the fittest" and "free enterprise" (meaning, in both cases, the irresponsible "right" to exploit the land and dominate and impoverish people) into which most Americans have been socialized by their education, the corporate-controlled media and politicians of both major parties, and the prevailing American economic structure that is based on and promotes that ideology and its consequences.

The steps proposed here are not exhaustive. People who are concerned about the earth community will use their experience and creativity to try them out, modify them or devise others to supplement or supplant some of them. In any event, the effort to conserve the trust of land must be undertaken if we are not to lose to a few or to oblivion our common inheritance.

chapter seven

The Spirit of the Earth

*　*　*

In our journey in rural America we have traveled both horizontally and vertically. We have traveled across the land and seen its changes. We have traveled through time and seen how some of those changes contradict our understanding of our American heritage and our religious tradition. We must now search to see if we can recover our past and struggle for our future in the present point of convergence between both. Our search will be aided if we can experience the earth as cocreature and then formulate ways in which to live harmoniously on and with it.

THE NATURE OF THE LAND

The casual traveler or tourist visiting one of the United States' national forests might be struck by the variety of people passing through a particular place. If that location includes a variety of hardwood trees, the traveler might wonder how different people see those trees. For example, a young oak tree might be viewed in contrasting ways by a lumber company executive, a carpenter and a traditional American Indian.

The lumber executive, concerned about harvesting faster-growing pine trees so as to obtain a quicker return on investment, might see the oak tree essentially as a large *weed.* If that executive were to hold a permit for harvesting lumber from this particular forest, the executive might recall that it was time to use another application of a special herbicide over part of the park, a herbicide that would selectively kill off all trees except the pines. In this way, the pines' fast growth could be accelerated even more, and so greater profits would be assured. The oak tree would be seen as little more than a barrier to businesses, an obstacle to progress.

The carpenter would see the young oak tree in a different way. For the carpenter the oak would be a potential *resource,* a future part of some furniture or cabinet or even a house frame. The oak as resource would be viewed as something to be carefully cultivated and then harvested at maturity. The tree would affect the carpenter's livelihood, as it did that of the lumber executive. For the carpenter, however, it is to be used in itself; it is not an object to be eliminated in order to acquire something else. It is seen as having value, a value that might be appropriated and added to through the transformative labor process once the tree is cut down. The tree is seen as lifeless, or as a lower life form that is intended for the proper use of the highest life form on earth, humanity. The oak tree would be seen as a natural resource, an aid to human progress.

The traditional American Indian would see the young oak tree as a *co-inhabitor* of Mother Earth, a living being to be appreciated and respected as another creature of God, the Great Spirit. It is not to be cut down while living; it can be used for shelter or heat only when it dies. The tree, for the American Indian, is to be treated as an equal being. It has value in itself and it has a right to life. And just as human beings in dying give their bodies for the rejuvenation of the earth, so, too, does the tree in dying give its body for the earth's rejuvenation or for the shelter or fuel needed by other of the earth's creatures.

In a similar way, perspectives on other aspects of the land might differ. Fertile agricultural land lying over coal beds might be seen as an "overburden" (a barrier to be removed) by a miner, as tax-producing property by a county commissioner, or as fertile and fragile soil by a farmer. In a similar way, too, might people view a human characteristic such as intelligence. For some it will be used primarily to dominate other people, to exercise power over them; for others it will be used primarily for personal benefit, to improve personal status or well-being; and for yet others, it will be used in the service of the entire community (which includes others and self). These different perspectives represent contrasting and conflicting understandings of creation and of humanity's relation to it. They demonstrate views of creation as *matter,* as *gift* and as *trust;* and the way that the earth and its creatures are perceived influences the property relations that govern it and the care that is taken of it.

When land is seen as *matter,* the primary attitude toward it is that it is to be *exploited* to serve the needs and wants of the exploiters, whether an individual or a nation. The property relationship then established is that land is an owned object. It exists solely to benefit the one who has civil title to it. Such a perspective is fundamentally *atheistic:* first, because it does not recognize that *the land is ultimately God's,* and therefore is not the owned object of anyone else; second, because it does not yield to the corollary of God's dominion: *people are God's stewards of the land,* and are to act in God's best interests— which means in the best interests of *all* of God's children, to whom the land has been willed by their Creator; and third, because it does not recognize that *God dwells in the earth* through nature, natural processes that God has set in motion. This perspective is also *anti-social:* it denies that the land is the common heritage of humanity, sees it solely in terms of the self and its desires, and uses it to the self's satisfaction.

When land is seen as *gift,* the primary attitude toward it is that it is to be *developed* or *ordered* to serve the needs both of the one who has control over it and of others of his or her generation. The one who receives a gift might dispose of it as he or she deems appropriate. The property relationship established here, too, is that land is an owned object, but its use is controlled more carefully than when land is seen as mere matter. For the one who sees land as a gift has a greater sense of physical and economic dependence upon it. The exploiter feels the luxury of wealth and power, while the recipient of a gift senses the responsibility of conserving the gift, recognizing its fragile nature and limited availability. In this perspective, the land exists primarily to benefit the one who has civil title to it or control over it: this is an *agnostic* perspective. The agnostic, unsure of his or her belief, vacillates between recognition of the land as God's creation and the land as material given, between a sense of stewardship and a sense of proprietorship, between a feeling of the presence of God in the land and a feeling of the absence of God in the land. This perspective is *asocial:* it neither denies nor affirms the land as having social intent and value, and develops and orders it according to the needs of the self primarily and society secondarily.

When the land is seen as a *trust,* the primary attitude toward it is that it is to be *cared* for and sometimes *ordered* to serve the needs of the human family (which includes the caretaker), other life forms and the earth itself, for present and future generations. The one who holds something in trust is aware that its well-being and the well-being of others depends on how he or she fulfills that trust. The one who holds something in trust knows that the entrustment is for a particular place and time, is not absolute and must be accounted for: it is local, temporal and temporary, and the trustee is accountable for it. The property relationship established here is that the land is a mortgaged subject; it has worth in and of itself, independent of the value placed on it by the one who holds title to it, because *it is,* because *it is of God,* and/or because *it is of humanity as a whole.* The land is seen as being on loan from the earth itself, from God, and/or from the human family: it has a social mortgage, and the trustee is its steward on behalf of those others (who include the steward as part of nature, as a member of the human family, and as a child of God within whom the Spirit of God dwells). In this perspective, the land exists primarily for the other, the others, or the Other, within all of whom, as a member of their respective communities, the trustee is living and is in relation. This perspective is fundamentally *theistic,* because the ultimate dominion of God is acknowledged either directly in a faith response or indirectly in a humanistic response that carries within it every sense of the being placed within and indwelt by the Spirit, but without an actualized faith in the Spirit. The humanist who has this perspective is not "a believer who doesn't realize that he or she believes," but rather a human being living in every respect as a child of God, conscious of the work of God and living the role of God's steward, but without recognizing the existence of God: one who is portrayed in a different context in Matthew's Gospel asking "When did I see you hungry, or thirsty, or naked, or homeless, or sick or in prison?" The end result of the actions of either the believer or the humanist is that in word and/or deed the work of God is carried on in both cases by those who understand themselves to be in some way entrusted with the land as its stewards. This perspective, then, is also fundamentally *social:* the steward recognizes that the land has great inherent value and communal value, and the needs of the community are primary. Again, the steward is part of that community, and so does not divide needs into "primary" and "secondary." Where the land is ordered it is done so out of necessity and not out of caprice or greed. And necessity does not only mean to support the human family; the ordering of nature by that part of nature entrusted with nature might be on behalf of any of the parts of nature. The land's trustees might have to intervene to prevent an irreversible scar from maiming the earth or to restore exploited areas, to preserve wildlife habitats, ecological balances, or scenic beauty, and to save life forms from extinction or decimation. The responsibilities of stewardship are many; the practitioners of stewardship are few.

The differing perspectives on the nature of the land are not exclusive categories within which people are confined. Rather, a person might shift back and forth between or among the categories, a movement usually dependent on insight into the implications of the different perspectives or on changing individual exigencies or desires. For example, a farmer might believe the land to be entrusted to his or her care, but be caught at the same time by low prices for agricultural products and high interest rates, and so eliminate terraces that prevent erosion in order to plant more crops. If the economic situation were to change, the farmer would feel more comfortable, and financially able to reject short-term gains in favor of long-term care of the land. Or someone who lives in a city or suburb and takes good care of his or her property might demand more and more electrical power because of the ever-widening array of consumer gadgets that become available and desired, and not consider that, for that need to be satisfied, utility corporations would try to justify potentially or actually harmful nuclear plants, farmland would be taken from production, and the energy resources of his or her children for the future would be depleted. If that person were to realize those effects of consumerism, he or she might try to support stewardship of all resources and not just the particular property under his or her care. The perspective closest to both the American heritage and, more especially, the Christian tradition is that of *seeing the land as a sacred and social trust.*

THREE BASIC PRINCIPLES

If we understand the land to be a sacred and social trust, then we should guide our interaction with the earth by basic principles of land relations. I would suggest three principles that embody the concept of land as trust and, moreover, are truly compatible both with our Christian tradition and with our American heritage. The "Principles of Land Relations" are:

1. The land is God's.

2. The land is entrusted to humanity.

3. The land is to be shared equitably through the ages.

These principles embody to a great extent, I believe, the "Principles of Land Stewardship" in *Strangers and Guests,* religious understandings of the nature of the earth, and the thrust of American (and international communitarian) ethical traditions of land justice theory and practice.

1. The land is God's: The earth and all in, on and around the earth are the Creator's. God, the Great Spirit, has domain over the entire universe, of which the earth is only a small part. But to say "the land is God's" does not mean that God's relation to the earth is to be understood in the same sense as when we say, "That house is mine," or "That pen is mine." In those cases, the item mentioned is just an object. It has some beneficial value for us, and we hope to have it as long as we need it, but there is not a close relationship to it, no matter that we live and love in the former or, holding the latter, express our deepest thoughts and longings. In contrast, God's relation to God's earth *is* a caring relation. God created the earth, and has the loving concern of a parent for it. God became enfleshed on the earth, and experienced first-hand the relation of the creature for its Creator. God contains the finite earth within infinite Being, and so God's Spirit permeates the earth. The earth is of the transcendent God, but the earth also is of the immanent God. And because the land is God's, it can never be appropriated, but only received in trust, by God's creatures. And because it is held in trust, it can never be destroyed or devastated by its caretakers, the human family that shares it and to whom it is entrusted.

2. The land is entrusted to humanity: People have been appointed by God to be the caretakers and guardians, the stewards and trustees, of the land. We who are made in God's image have the (literally) sacred task of being co-creators with God of an earth ever in process as it experiences ever new generations in itself and in the life forms that inhabit it. We are entrusted with the earth and we must care for the earth. We must *care* for it in that we must take care of it, exercising our stewardship in a way that conserves it and promotes the global sharing of its fruits. We must care for it in that we are concerned about its well-being, and are working to promote its internal harmony and the harmony of its inhabitants among themselves and to it. We must care for it, finally, in that we struggle against its exploitation by others, striving both to help them change their perspective about the nature of the land

and simultaneously to prevent, to the extent that we are able, its selfish appropriation and despoilation. In order to fulfill our role as trustees of the earth we must both care for that part of it over which we exercise stewardship, and catalyze care for that part of it which is under others' control.

3. *The land is to be shared equitably through the ages:* The earth, entrusted to humanity's care, is not given solely for humanity's use. The caretakers of the land are to promote the well-being of the earth as an interrelated community of land and lives. In practice, this means overseeing an equitable distribution of the land and its fruits among all the members of every generation. This distribution must be based on the recognition of God's ultimate dominion over the earth and of the status of the earth and all of its inhabitants as creatures of God. In practice, this does not mean that humanity must strive to promote the well-being of every other living creature; each living being, each species (including the human family), is responsible for the continuation of its own kind, and each is governed by its genetic constitution, relates to its own environment (which includes hostile life forms and earth movements) and is ruled by the laws of nature created by God. One of those laws requires that life give way to other life (other creatures or new members of the same creature). The ultimate trust of humanity is to see, as far as possible, that the balance of the earth is not threatened—especially by humanity itself—to the extent that few or no life forms can survive and sustain themselves. The laws and balance of nature require that all that lives must die (this includes inanimate beings, such as planets and stars, as well as animate beings, plants, animals and people) and be transformed (into energy, into inanimate matter, or, for people, into a new form of conscious life with a heightened and continual awareness of God). The earth shifts and changes and its life forms change. The land experiences earthquakes, volcanoes, tidal waves, tornadoes, floods and drought. Species of animal and plant life evolve and then become extinct. Within species, each generation gives way to a new generation. Through all of this, humanity, since its emergence at a very rudimentary level to its present more highly sophisticated level

of intelligence, has been charged with the responsibility of caring for the environment in which it was born or into which it migrated. People have not always fulfilled this responsibility. They have fallen away from obedience to God; they have passively ignored or actively violated the trust given to them by God to care for the earth, the garden of God into which God placed them. Consequently, the earth and they suffered from the disruption of the harmony that God placed in creation, a harmony dependent upon each creature fulfilling its role. In the incarnation the harmony is restored, humanity becomes obedient to God, and the God-Man is able dramatically to exercise control over the elements, illness and even death itself (while yet himself being subject to this latter part of the natural cycle). The possibility is renewed for those who have negated God and their role in his world to take up their responsibility as caretakers of the earth. Their responsibility, again, is to ensure that the land and its resources are distributed *equitably*, taking into account the *needs* of the earth, and that this equitable distribution be *generational*, extending through time; each generation must see itself as part of the total age of humanity, and be conscious of and make provision for the earth's needs in the present and in the future, as much as can be foreseen. Humanity's acceptance of this responsibility implies its awareness of the holistic balance that is the earth, including humanity as part of the interrelated whole, and human commitment to preserving that balance, now and in the future.

THE SPIRIT OF THE EARTH

God has created us; the earth gives us life. We are, then, children of God and children of Mother Earth. We are part of that totality of creation that emanated from God; we are part of that community of relation that is rooted in the earth. Yet, we are unique in both cases. Although part of creation, we are the only part made in God's image and likeness and the only part appointed to be co-creators and trustees of the earth. Although part of the integrated community that is the earth, we are, as is every part, genetically distinct and having our own physical and social needs and species destiny. Our religious dimension adds another aspect of uniqueness to us: we are the only part of the physical creation that is conscious of being created by God and that can acknowledge its gratitude to and love for God. Other parts of creation testify unknowingly to the knowledge and power and love of God; we do so consciously. We are also able, consciously, to understand the forces at work in the earth, the laws of nature implanted by God, and to discern disruptions in those laws, caused by members of the earth community. We who are Christian can come to an understanding, through that awareness of nature, of what traditional American Indians mean when they say "Mother Earth," and know why they treat the earth with reverence and respect.

With our acknowledgement of God as Creator and our perception of God's order at work in the world, we can understand what is meant by the *Spirit* of the earth and the *spirit* of the earth.

The *Spirit* of the earth is God, the Great Spirit, the transcendent yet immanent One who created the world, restored its relation to its Creator, and continually renews that relation. When we acknowledge the Spirit of the earth we acknowledge God's dominion over and presence in the earth. This acknowledgement means that we recognize that God's Spirit alone is the earth's ultimate guide, and we place ourselves in the position of God's stewards and trustees, with all that that implies.

Most of us think only of God's *transcendence* when we consider the relation of God to creation. We see God as the Creator distinct from the works of creation. We see God as the Lord of all that is. We see God as a loving Father, in the imagery Jesus used. We see God as the great Judge, knowing our sinfulness and our goodness and one day calling us to an accounting for our lives. In all of these images, God is external to us; God is the Other, even if we address God by the intimate term of "Father." What we frequently do not consider (except for experts in and practitioners of "spirituality") is that God is also *immanent,* within us and all of creation. St. Paul reminds us of the God within us when he says, "You are the temple of the living God" (2 Corinthians 6:16); or, "Are you not aware that you are the temple of God, and that the Spirit of God dwells in you?" (1 Corinthians 3:16); or, "Perhaps you yourselves do not realize that Christ Jesus is in you" (2 Corinthians 13:5). When we think about God's immanence, God dwelling in us, we realize how much more intimate and personal is our relationship with God. God is as close to us as we are to ourselves. If we allow ourselves to transcend time and experience the immanent God, we will know first-hand the Spirit of the earth that is in us. We will know how we are "strangers and guests" on the land—not only because of its ultimate ownership by God, but because in God we have our lasting abode. In experiencing the Spirit of the earth, we are one in spirit with others, sharing our sense of God's immanence, despite cultural variations in how we describe it. For example, our experience of God's immanence is similar, in our American context, with the experience of the traditional American Indians, who on meditating see and experience God in creation. Our sense of God's immanence also aids our understanding of our role as God's stewards and the earth's trustees. We know that we are pilgrims on the earth, we know that we are God's images, we know that our life is brief in the timeline of time. We are able then to try to avoid consumerism and property possessiveness. We are able to see better how this fragile planet must be cared for as an earthen vessel in which God is, though not contained or confined. The Spirit of the earth, then, is the immanent God. And God within draws creation to its Creator, through loving guidance of the land's trustees and through the natural rhythms and forces placed in creation itself: the spirit of the earth.

The *spirit* of the earth is the spirit of creation itself, the potential placed in it by God to evolve toward God. The spirit of the earth is a reflection of God's immanence, of the Spirit of the earth; it is also an indication of God's imminence as ages pass and creation strains toward God, strains to have the spirit taken up into the Spirit: "All creation groans and is in agony"

(Romans 8:22) waiting for that ultimate union. The spirit of the earth is the earth ordering itself according to the laws and potential that God created in it at the dawn of time, and that converge it toward the Spirit within.

It is this sense of the earth, this spirit of the earth, that is personified by indigenous peoples as Mother Earth, the life-giver who helps people live and follow their calling. Mother Earth provides physical nourishment and spiritual understanding. She speaks through the elements, through other living creatures, and through dreams and visions. She represents a totality of being similar, in a way, to the scriptural understanding of the role of Jesus. For example, Paul wrote "Never censure an old man, but appeal to him as a father; you should treat younger men as brothers, older women as mothers, and younger women as sisters" (1 Timothy 5:1–2), teaching us that we are all family; Jesus told a crowd of people "These are my mother and brothers" (Mark 3:34), not to exclude his family relations from his circle of friends but to include his circle of friends in his family; and Paul taught "He is before all else that is. In him everything continues in being. . . .It pleased God to make absolute fullness reside in him, and, by means of him, to reconcile everything in his person, both on earth and in the heavens" (Colossians 1:17, 19), declaring that in Jesus all creation converges, is contained and is restored to a right relation with God. In Jesus, we would add, the Word became flesh, the Spirit of the earth became the spirit of the earth and the union catalyzed the final convergence of the two in the relations external to Jesus. In humanity, the spirit *reflects* the Spirit because people are God's images and God has become incarnated; and the spirit *approaches* the Spirit as people, part of creation and of the earth community, labor to offer creation to the Spirit. This interrelatedness of people and creation and God is similar to the Native Americans' consciousness of the earth's creatures as "all my relatives," and of Native Americans' perceptions of their role as guardians of Mother Earth, their need to respect her and their sense of her spiritual presence.

The spirit of the earth is the force of harmony and interrelatedness among the land's inhabitants. Harmony is a sense of place, a knowledge (on however much a rudimentary or instinctual level) of position. Interrelatedness is a sense of relation, of respective position on the land, of how a particular place relates to other particular places. In the spirit of the earth, life forms are generated, live, reproduce and die; they carry within themselves a genetic constitution (evolvable, usually due to external sources such as radiation or environmental alterations), the "seed of their own kind" (see Genesis 1), that is the basis for their life in the world. Some life forms serve others in a sacrificial way, as food: plants serve herbivores and omnivores, animals serve carnivores and omnivores. In this way their lives give life and new generations are given the opportunity of life and service.

The cycle of life goes on, and upward, too, in a spiral in which higher self-perceptions are developed, broader social integration and relation are achieved, and a closer union with the Spirit is approximated. We know of animals that use tools to achieve some particular objective (for example, one kind of woodpecker uses twigs to dislodge insects to satisfy its hunger), and that wash their food for reasons of taste (a biologist named Lyall Watson recorded that a female monkey on one of the islands of Japan washed a potato one day, liked the new taste better than the old, then taught the new behavior to the other monkeys). We know too that some form of collective unconscious exists, sometimes as an *instinct* (schools of fish and flocks of birds change direction simultaneously) and sometimes as an *intuition,* perhaps on a telepathic level (Watson observed on those Japanese islands a dramatically curious phenomenon: soon after the monkeys on the first island began washing their potatoes, monkeys on other islands started to do the same— *even though there was no contact among the islands*). The psychologist C. G. Jung theorized a collective unconscious; also, he and others studying dreams discovered symbols that recurred transculturally and transhistorically. As we discover all of this, we sense to an ever greater extent the spirit of the earth and the energy immanent in it, and the impetus toward God implanted in its laws.

The spirit of the earth draws the earth toward the Spirit of the earth. Sometimes it encounters resistance; in the areas of land ethics we have been discussing, for example, the spirit is thwarted temporarily by humanity's complacency before injustice or outright rejection of the spirit and the Spirit. But when we consciously live in and allow our lives to be guided by the spirit and the Spirit, we participate in the convergence of the two, and share in the union they have in Jesus Christ. We become more aware that it is in the Spirit that we live and move and have our being, that in the Spirit all things are one, and that we have been granted what Jesus prayed for shortly before his death: "That all may be one, as you Father, are in me, and I in you; I pray that they may be one in us" (John 17:21). We might move in and out of this consciousness, much as people's practices on the land might shift from their acting as trustees to their acting as exploiters, and so on. What we should strive for is to have a basic option for living with the spirit of the earth in the Spirit of the earth. Should we achieve this, we, too, will guide that part of the earth—land and people—which is our particular responsibility toward an ever closer participation in the life of the Spirit.

THE TRUST OF LAND AND THE FUTURE OF THE EARTH

Our journey across rural America and through its history has led us to the point of choosing a route for the future of the land. The route we choose will depend on how much we have understood our past, how we view our present, and what we envision as our future possibilities.

For the sake of the entire earth community, we must see the land as a trust from God and see ourselves as its trustees. If we accept that teaching from our religious tradition, we will be strengthened to struggle to care for the earth. If we reappropriate the stewardship tradition from our American heritage, we will have a geographical historical support for our proposals for our American context.

In the history of humanity, the stewardship role ordained

for us by God has frequently been rejected. In ages past, after the disobedience of the first members of the race, creation was fallen. People had sinned against their Creator and negated their stewardship role, and thus creation suffered from human selfishness and exploitation. As the Incarnation of God, Jesus Christ called us back to obedience to God, to acceptance of our place in nature as part of it and yet as caretakers for it. As part of it, we are to live in harmony with nature; as its caretakers we are to fulfill our ecological role in it (which includes for us, as images of God, caring for the land), thereby helping its harmony and balance to continue—much as every part of any ecological system is necessary to keep the whole system in balance, but with the unique addition of having far-reaching control and responsibility as God's stewards.

We must remember, as we care for this trust of land, that we are part of nature, and that natural beauty includes ourselves and the way we order nature—when we order it with respect for the earth and for other life forms. Humanity is capable of exploitation and destruction—but also of cultivation and construction. We cut down; but we plant, too.

Sometimes it might be an all too easy out for us to neglect our constructive role in nature and not see ourselves as part of nature and of the beauty of the earth. We use humanity's exploitation of the land in the past and present as a given for the future—and so we deny anew our own stewardship responsibility. We must accept ourselves as part of nature and not, as Wendell Berry points out in *The Unsettling of America,* see pictures of the natural world as beautiful only when people are not in them. And if we are part of nature, then we must responsibly live our lives in harmony with its other parts while fulfilling our role as trustees of the earth.

The land, again, is entrusted to us for all of us. The principles and practices described in this book permit either widespread individual civil ownership of the trust of land or community ownership of the land on behalf of every individual member of the community. In either case, selfish use of the land is negated. In either case, dominance of the few over the many—whether the few be wealthy capitalists or a party elite—is excluded. The fundamental proposal is that all of us as individuals, as community and as global human family, as children of God, should have a land base and a sense of responsibility for it. That land base can provide us with life's necessities and help us to control our individual and communal destiny.

The jazz musician Chuck Mangione has captured that sense of the land in his song "Children of Sanchez":

> Without dreams of hope and pride a man will die.
> Though his flesh still moves his heart sleeps in the grave;
> Without land man never dreams 'cause he's not free—
> All men need a place to live with dignity.
>
> Every child belongs to mankind's family,
> Children are the fruit of all humanity;
> Let them feel the love of all the human race,
> Touch them with the warmth, the strength of that embrace.

All of us, men and women, need a land base from which to support ourselves and be free to dream of a better future for the earth and our children. Our children are the children of the entire human family, and the way we share in the land and care for the land will determine the form of the land and the fate of our children.

The future of the earth depends on how we care for our trust of land. We have reached a fork in the road, a fork not unlike those reached time and again by our ancestors. In one direction we can see a difficult path, one that requires discipline and sacrifice, that gradually leads to an earth in harmony. In the other direction we can see an easier path, one allowing consumerism and complacency, that shortly leads to an earth torn by strife among people and with people.

In some ways our choice is different from that presented to past generations. We have had now, for some forty years, the power to destroy the earth entirely in a nuclear war. We now manufacture, more so than in the past, toxic substances that pollute air, land and water. We now deplete the earth's resources at a far more rapid rate than was possible for past generations. Therefore, the very future of the earth is at stake today, to the extent that the path we choose will determine whether or not the earth will survive the acts of our generation.

The earth and our children await our decision.